How to Change the Games Children Play

Second Edition

G. S. Don Morris
California State
Polytechnic University
Pomona, California

Illustrated by
Mark Sullivan

Burgess Publishing Company
Minneapolis, Minnesota

Consulting editors

Eloise M. Jaeger
University of Minnesota
Minneapolis, Minnesota

Robert M. Clayton
Colorado State University
Fort Collins, Colorado

Copyright © 1980, 1976 by Burgess Publishing Company
Printed in the United States of America
Library of Congress Catalog Number 79-56429
ISBN 0-8087-3967-0

Burgess Publishing Company
7108 Ohms Lane
Minneapolis, Minnesota 55435

0 9 8 7 6 5 4 3 2 1

To Pat, Kari, and Peter

THE FAMILY CIRCUS.   By Bil Keane

"We made it up ourselves. You don't need nine
guys on a team, or grownups, or uniforms. . . .
It's like baseball, only better!"

Contents

Foreword to the First Edition

This book is different. Instead of the usual game-books which contain descriptions of games and generalized statements of philosophy, this book presents the thesis that the very structure of the game must be analyzed in terms of the specific objective sought — "specific outcome behaviors".

This is an interesting and an important notion. It asks teachers to look at games *before* they use them in their programs, rather than attaching *values* to the games as justification for use; values that may not be there due to the very structure of the game.

The second notion of the book, and equally important for educational use of games, is the plea for alternatives and changes in the structure of games. This, Dr. Morris suggests, will include more students. The exclusion of students who *need* to participate will be diminished and perhaps will even disappear.

Dr. Morris offers a model for the analysis of games and guidelines for discovering and creating new ones. These operational tools can serve an excellent means for the teacher who has to interpret models into practical ways of "doing it."

Throughout the book the author projects a sense of respect for the individual's ability to think, to feel, to make decisions and to cooperate with others — to join together in both the analysis and design of games and the sheer enjoyment of playing them.

Muska Mosston

Preface

This book is designed for everyone who teaches games to children—elementary and secondary teachers, physical educators, special educators, and recreation directors.

It is important to clarify a few points that have been raised by readers of the first edition. The term *behavior*, as used in this book, refers only to the observed performances of game players by game leaders. This means that the term *behavior* incorporates such items as the number of players actually moving in a game, how long they are allowed to move, where they move, and the quality and efficiency with which they move. A major concept presented in the book is that the game structure can influence the effectiveness of the behavior that occurs in a game. In addition to the kinds of behavior identification above, there are many other types of behavior that the teacher or game leader can identify. This book presents a model that will help game designers design, develop, and analyze games as they are played. Games are, of course, just *one* medium teachers can use to teach children more about themselves.

There have been several changes in this second edition. The games analysis model has been expanded to explain further the structure of movement games. The expanded model is much easier for any game designer to use than the old model. I also introduce another concept, known as the "games analysis process," which serves as a strategy for engaging players in the analysis and design of games. Many other uses for the games analysis process are suggested, too. Public Law 94-142 has been operational for several years. Teachers and recreators must be able to include many different skill levels in a single game form. This edition helps game designers incorporate all skill abilities into one game and demonstrates how one can match movement tasks to developmental skill levels. Another chapter provides strategies that help game participants become more skillful (i.e., improve the efficiency of their movements). Finally, many new games have been added to the book—games to promote skill development and games just for fun.

I have attempted to retain all of the positive aspects of the first edition and have added to and improved the original concepts. I don't believe that the games analysis model is the *only* model that allows us to examine games. As a matter of fact, I hope it will lead many of you to create your own models that will be tailored to your specific needs.

I wish to thank my elementary students in Eugene, Oregon, and in Bozeman, Montana, and in Diamond Bar, California, for demonstrating to me that the games analysis concept really does work. And I want to thank my high school students in Upland, California, for prompting me to reconsider what games really do to students. The many teachers who have used these ideas also receive my thanks—it is because of their comments that this edition is possible. Special thanks are extended to Vicki Cowett for typing and otherwise assisting with the manuscript. Mark Sullivan's drawings have received many plaudits from the readers of the first edition, and his work is much appreciated. Finally, my family deserves my praise—their patience and input made this book possible.

G. S. Don Morris
California State Polytechnic University
Pomona

Chapter

Introduction to Games Analysis

People of all ages play games—many of us play games our entire lives, while others of us feel that games are played only by the young. As we enter the 1980s, we find that more and more people are playing games throughout their lifetime as more leisure time becomes available. Recently there has been a fairly significant boom within the games community, making the games business a contributor to everyone's lifestyle.

Games exist in many forms. This book will focus upon games that require physical movements, such as those found in sports, physical education classes, and recreational settings. Within each one of these settings, games tend to be played for specific purposes. For example, we often engage in movement games so we can: (1) learn how to move more efficiently, (2) learn team strategies, (3) learn how to interact socially with our peers, (4) experience a feeling of self-worth, (5) spend some time with friends, and (6) play and simply have fun. Certainly we play games for many other reasons that you, the reader, can identify.

The author believes that the game leaders (i.e., teachers, recreation leaders, coaches, or anyone who has designed a game) need to understand that the design and/or structure of a game seems to contribute a great deal to the kinds of experiences the participants have while playing a game. Unless a game leader understands that it is necessary to attend to the structure of a game, the performance outcome experienced by the participants will not necessarily match the initially stated or desired purpose of game play.

Within the educational community, educators use games as a means to an end. During the 1960's and even through much of the 1970's, it was popular for many writers to criticize the direction games were heading. Certainly this author cast a few stones in that direction. However, criticism or constant evaluation of programs is not necessarily unhealthy. Those of us who use games to promote specific educational goals and objectives should constantly analyze what we are doing for and to our students or game participants. We need a tool that permits us to evaluate games and their outcomes.

A concept known as games analysis provides games teachers, and for that matter all teachers, with a model that can help them develop games designed to meet the needs of both leaders and participants. Since the introduction of the games analysis (g.a.) model in 1976, many games leaders across the United States have used it in many different ways. Physical educators have used games analysis to design game and sport activities commensurate with the skills of their students; special educators have used the model to enhance the mainstreaming concept; and recreation leaders have found it useful in designing new and enjoyable games for people of all ages.

GAMES ANALYSIS—A MODEL
AND A PROCESS

The games analysis model attempts to provide a framework in which all movement games can be described and thus analyzed. The original games analysis model was presented in very simple terms. Since 1976 the author has expanded the model to assist game designers with their analyses of movement games. By no means is this model an absolute—rather, it is expected that many other people will add to or delete items from the model, thus developing their own model. The concept that is of paramount importance is that game designers must critically analyze a game's design in relation to its stated purpose and to the actual performance of the participants. What follows is a model that has met the needs of this author as well as hundreds of other games leaders and players. It is hoped that the remaining pages provide a sound and practical working tool that can be used by all game designers.

INITIAL MODEL

All movement games seem to possess players, equipment, rules, organizational patterns, movements, and rationales for playing. Several authors have suggested that games are made up of many different categories.* The initial games analysis model has six categories: players, equipment, movement, organizational patterns, limitations, and purposes. Each category comprises a number of components. A concrete description of any movement game can now be demonstrated. The games analysis model (Table 1-1) shows a variety of randomly chosen components placed in the appropriate categories. Game components are nothing more than additional game descriptors. The model allows the game designer to study any game he or she wishes to analyze and to assign the game's components to the appropriate categories. Once this has been accomplished, it is possible to provide a wide range of uses of the model to all games designers, many of which are educational, as well as recreational by design.

COMPLEX MODEL

The old games analysis model has been expanded in response to requests from game designers all over this counrty for more information to facilitate the analysis of games and thereby lead to more effective use of the g.a. model. What follows, then, is the newer model with explanations and descriptions of the categories (Table 1-2).

Before proceeding to an explanation of each category, it must be said that the model is dynamic and constantly evolving. The purpose of forming game categories is for ease of discussion and explanation—no doubt some components within the stated categories may overlap. It is the interaction effect of all the categories that results in a game.

---

*See, for example, Victor P. Dauer and Robert P. Pangrazi, *Dynamic Physical Education for Elementary School Children*, 6th edition (Minneapolis: Burgess Publishing Company, 1979); Glen Kirschner, *Physical Education for Elementary School Children*, 4th edition (Dubuque, Iowa: William C. Brown Company, 1978): E. Mauldon and H. B. Redfern, *Games Teaching* (London: MacDonald and Evans, 1970); and Muska Mosston, *Teaching Physical Education* (Columbus, Ohio: Charles E. Merrill Company, 1966).

TABLE 1-1.
GAMES ANALYSIS MODEL—CATEGORIES AND COMPONENTS

Players	Equipment	Movement Pattern	Organizational Pattern	Limitations	Purpose
individual	balls	running	random placement	3 outs per inning	To win
2 per team	bats	jumping	circle	10 yds for 1st down	To promote cooperative behavior
3 per team	sticks	hopping	columns	boundaries on field	Help develop locomotor skills
4 per team	gloves	skipping	double circles	5 min. per quarter	Promotes problem-solving behavior
5 per team	hoops	walking	files	tag below waist	Aids in eye-hand coordination
six on one team, four on another	plastic bottles	galloping	double columns	only 5 players per team	Helps develop self concept
even number on one team, odd number on other	ropes	kicking	staggered file	4 downs to make a T.D.	Develop competitive spirit
	bases	throwing	even/odd file	must dribble the ball for every step taken	Promotes sportsmanship
???	wands	catching	diamond	???	Develop cardiovascular fitness
	bowling pins	twisting	triangle		
	individual body parts	rolling	square		
	???	???	???		

TABLE 1-2.
COMPLEX GAMES ANALYSIS MODEL

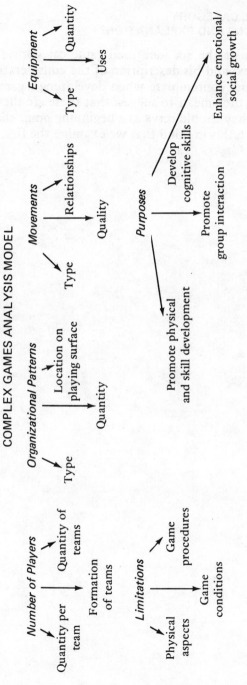

**INDIVIDUAL CATEGORY
DESCRIPTIONS AND EXPLANATIONS**

For each of the six identified game categories, the author has chosen to expand his description of the considerations every game designer must contemplate when developing a game. By no means does the author mean to suggest that these are the only considerations, but they should serve as a beginning point that can be added to. It is with this in mind that we examine the first game category, *Number of Players* (Table 1-3).

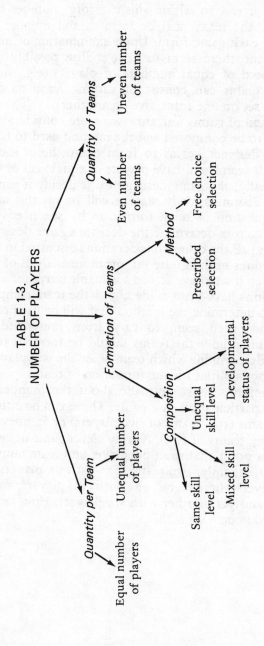

TABLE 1-3.
NUMBER OF PLAYERS

Explanation: There are at least three considerations a game designer must attend to within this category: number of players per team, how the teams will be formed, and number of teams formed within each game form. Upon examination of quantity of players per team, there seem to exist endless possibilities: teams can be composed of equal numbers of players (e.g., five players per team) or teams can consist of varying numbers of players per team (e.g., six on one team, five on another).

The formation of teams warrants two more considerations: how the teams are to be composed and the method used to form them. When a game designer begins to form teams, he or she needs to determine if all teams will have players of equal skill or of varying skill. Additionally, the game designer must decide if game players of similar or dissimilar body stature will be on the same team. Finally, the question of team formation by sex needs to be resolved. Many factors determine the decisions game designers make about these and all the other considerations discussed in this book. If this model does nothing else but promote analysis of the games we all play, then it will have served a valuable purpose.

Once decisions have been made about the team composition, it is necessary to determine the method that will be used to form the teams. Methods used seem to vary from prescribed selection (someone dictates how the teams should be formed) to the individual player determining which team he or she will play on. There exist endless possibilities for the formation of teams.

Finally, decisions must be made about the number of teams necessary for participation in a game. There can be either an even number of teams (two teams of five players) or an uneven number of teams (three teams of five). A truly clever game designer would suggest at this point that multiple player and team numbers could also exist (for example, two teams, one with six players, the other with four players; three teams, one with two players, another with five players, and yet another with six players. How many combinations can you come up with?

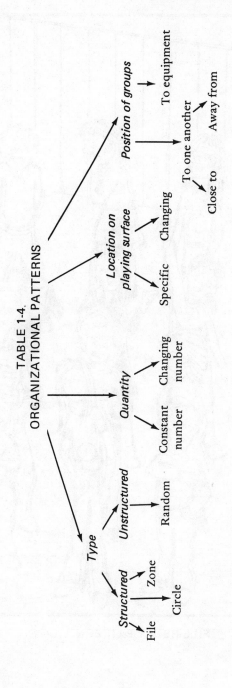

TABLE 1-4.
ORGANIZATIONAL PATTERNS

FILE RELAY PATTERN

Explanation: Within a single game the players and/or teams of players can be found in a multitude of positions on the playing surface. The type of patterns varies from very structured patterns (file, circle, zone, etc.) to unstructured patterns (random). In some games the patterns used remain constant, as in a relay (four teams standing in separate columns), or the patterns change as seen in basketball (zone defenses or man-to-man defenses).

By design, teams are often relegated to specific locations on the playing surface, as evidenced in a game like volleyball. However, strategies of all games suggest that teams and/or players shift their locations relative to one another, to the equipment, or to game boundaries (Table 1-4).

TABLE 1-5.
MOVEMENTS

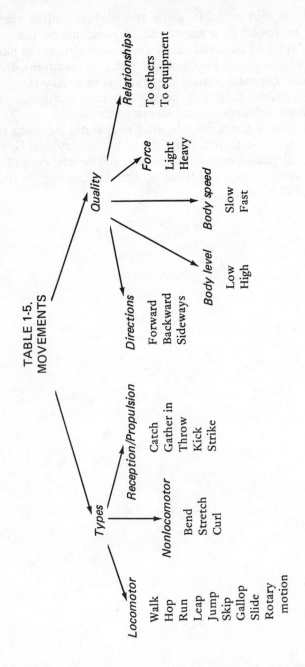

Types

Locomotor

Walk
Hop
Run
Leap
Jump
Skip
Gallop
Slide
Rotary
motion

Nonlocomotor

Bend
Stretch
Curl

Reception/Propulsion

Catch
Gather in
Throw
Kick
Strike

Quality

Relationships

To others
To equipment

Force

Light
Heavy

Body speed

Slow
Fast

Body level

Low
High

Directions

Forward
Backward
Sideways

Explanation: All movement games involve various types of physical movements that are performed independently of one another or in combination with one another. The types of movements include locomotor (walk, hop, run, etc.), nonlocomotor (bend, stretch, curl, etc.), and reception/propulsion (catch, throw, kick, etc.) skills. Game designers need to understand that movements are performed in various directions (forward, backward, sideways), at different body levels, and at a variety of speeds and forces. The game limits, purposes, or internal demands seem to mandate which movements occur. It is possible that the game designer can dictate the kinds of movements to be performed, or the designer can simply allow movements to happen within the game. Regardless of the movements that do occur during the game, it is important to understand that they are always performed in relationship to other people. Certainly the skill level of the performers, as well as the environmental limits where the game is played, influence what will and will not occur during the game. Even game strategies and conditions affect the type and quality of movements viewed during game time. As with the previously discussed game categories, a multitude of possibilities exists (Table 1-5).

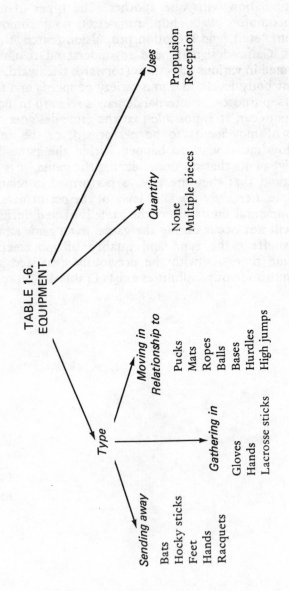

TABLE 1-6.
EQUIPMENT

Type

Sending away

Bats
Hocky sticks
Feet
Hands
Racquets

Gathering in

Gloves
Hands
Lacrosse sticks

*Moving in
Relationship to*

Pucks
Mats
Ropes
Balls
Bases
Hurdles
High jumps

Quantity

None
Multiple pieces

Uses

Propulsion
Reception

Explanation: There are several types of equipment. There is equipment that allows players to *send away* other pieces of equipment (bats, feet, hands, racquets, etc.), and there is equipment that allows players *to receive* or *gather in* objects traveling towards them (gloves, hands, lacrosse sticks, etc.). Players also move in relationship to small equipment (e.g., balls, hoops, ropes) as well as to large equipment (e.g., pommel horses, trampolines, high jumps).

Game designers make decisions about the number of equipment pieces used in a game. It is possible to use just players, without any equipment, or it is possible to use one or more pieces of equipment. The decision to use or not to use equipment depends on the ability of the players, the geographic area the game is played in, the availability of equipment, and the purpose of the game.

Finally, game designers need to determine how the equipment should be used. Contrary to popular opinion, the same equipment can be used in a variety of ways. For example, a badminton racquet can be used in the traditional manner or it can be swung as a baseball bat (striking at a "bird," paper ball, small nerf ball). Hula hoops can be used as bases or as jumping devices. With just a little imagination one can develop multiple uses for all equipment. Not only can equipment be used to receive and propel, but it can be used for . . . *your ideas*. . . . The number of possibilities seems endless (Table 1-6).

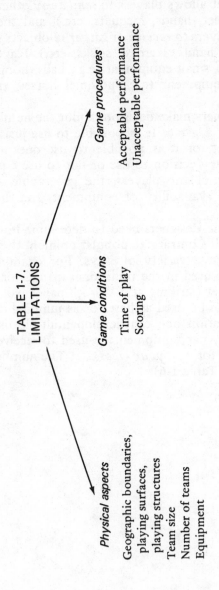

TABLE 1-7.
LIMITATIONS

Physical aspects

Geographic boundaries,
playing surfaces,
playing structures
Team size
Number of teams
Equipment

Game conditions

Time of play
Scoring

Game procedures

Acceptable performance
Unacceptable performance

Explanation: Limitations, or rules, include the physical limits that exist for every game form. In many instances game designers can control the physical limits, but it is quite possible that these limits have been predetermined, either out of necessity or by design. It is important in many games to define the geographic boundaries within which the players must stay. Sometimes it is necessary or desirable to modify the playing surfaces and structures in which, or on which, the game is played. Restrictions are also placed upon the number and size of teams allowed within a single game form, and choices are made about the formation of teams. Many games have restrictions on the equipment used (size, shape) and on the quantity of equipment pieces allowed (e.g., one basketball).

Decisions are also made about game conditions (i.e., scoring and time of play). Again, many choices can be made within this subcategory. Finally, game procedures are outlined within the limitations category. The procedures identify acceptable and unacceptable performance within a single game form. For example, in "regulation" basketball it is permissible to shoot the ball with one or two hands, but it is not permissible to "travel" with the ball or to "foul" another player (Table 1-7).

As with all of the other game categories, it is perfectly acceptable for you to add your own subcategories.

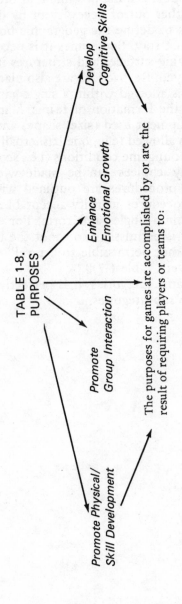

TABLE 1-8.
PURPOSES

Develop
Cognitive Skills

Enhance
Emotional Growth

Promote
Group Interaction

Promote Physical/
Skill Development

The purposes for games are accomplished by or are the
result of requiring players or teams to:

Understand that they are unique individuals.
Win.
Interact with one another.
Score most points.
Obtain highest score.
Obey the rules.
Share with others.

Explanation: People play games for a multitude of reasons. Generally, they engage in games to promote specific physical or skill development, such as improving their ability to control body parts or equipment. In addition, people want to enjoy themselves while playing with other people. Some games are designed to promote problem-solving skills as well as enhance basic cognitive abilities. To make sure that games serve their stated purpose, game designers must think critically about the reasons for engaging people in a variety of game forms (Table 1-8).

The complex games analysis model allows one to understand the components of all movement games. Some people have likened the model to a recipe that game designers can use to concoct many different kinds of games. The model is applicable to any group of individuals who engage in game play. Games analysis, as a concept, can assist all game designers with the design, alteration, adaptation, or modification of any movement game form so that the needs and motor status of all performers can be accommodated.

GAMES ANALYSIS GRID

To aid game designers, a games analysis grid has been devised to help in the analysis of games and sports. The grid simply lists the six categories of a game and provides a space for the game title and game descriptors. The game designers can place the given game's component descriptors in the appropriate categories. A typical grid, definitely incomplete, for two games of basketball is shown on the following page, illustrating the manipulation of one game category—organizational pattern. It demonstrates how the game of basketball can be described by placing its components in the appropriate categories. The grid becomes a formula for the game of basketball; i.e., using the stated components within the categories one begins to play the game.

Initially you will find it necessary to include in the grid a section that verbally describes how one would play the game. After a period of time it may no longer be necessary to include this section as you will find it quite easy to describe the game by simply reading across the grid categories. It is important to understand that the description section is not a necessary category that affects the use of the games analysis concept—it is simply an aid to folks who are just beginning to use the games analysis model. The example used also demonstrates a specific use of the grid—keep all categories constant, change one or more components in one category, and you have another basketball *type* game. More regarding this procedure will be found in the next chapter.

Changing, adapting, or designing a game should be accomplished while keeping specific educational outcomes in mind. If you want specific motor activities to be enhanced the games must be designed to account for the current growth and development status of the performers; in addition you must have the knowledge to examine other factors that may influence the youngsters' ability to perform the task. An example of this is found within the game of T-ball baseball.

In T-ball baseball, the baseball is placed upon a stationary batting tee and the batter strikes the ball off of the tee. T-ball is played with youngsters eight years and younger. Now, this game takes into consideration the youngster's current stage of growth and development; at the same time it identifies a factor that influences performance of the striking motor behavior. The eight-and-under youngster's visual-perceptual

TABLE 1-9.
GAMES ANALYSIS GRID

Name of Game	Players	Equipment	Movement Pattern	Purpose	Organizational Pattern	Limitations	Description
1. Basketball	5 per team	1 basketball	running, jumping shooting	score most points	zone	NCAA rules	A brief game description would follow
2. Basketball	5 per team	1 basketball	running, jumping shooting	score most points	man-man	NCAA rules	A brief game description would follow

apparatus is far from mature in terms of tracking a moving object. Research indicates that youngsters of this age can more efficiently track horizontally and vertically moving balls than balls that travel in a large arc. Thus T-ball, by design, allows for this behavior to a degree by utilizing a batting tee. In addition the game has identified two factors that influence whether or not the youngsters can successfully strike the ball. We call them the method of trajectory factor and the angle of trajectory factor. We know that youngsters eight years old and under can hit a stationary ball in the horizontal plane more efficiently than a ball which is moving in a variety of planes. This last concept is known as task analysis. Certainly elimination of the pitcher may "save" young players' arms as well as speed up the offensive part of the game.

The grid can help game designers as they develop new games, describe existing games, or modify and alter game forms to achieve specific game performance outcomes.

USE OF GAMES ANALYSIS MODEL AND GRID

It is possible to use the model as an aid in designing a game. Examining the new, more complex model, a game designer must make decisions about the number of players to be incorporated into a game form. The g.a. model attempts to identify for the game designer the kind of decisions that need to be made in the number of players category (i.e., number per team, formation of teams, and numbers of teams) as well as the decisions necessary in the remaining five categories. In other words, the game designer can make decisions about the components of each game category by using the model and placing the appropriate descriptors on the g.a. grid under the correct heading. If the games analysis model is used in this manner, new game designers will find it fairly easy to develop their own "new" games or to modify existing games. The remaining chapters in this book share with you many other uses of the games analysis concept.

References

Kirchner, Glenn. *Physical Education for Elementary School Children,* 4th Ed. Dubuque, Iowa: William C. Brown Co., 1978.

Mauldon, E., and Redfern, H. B. *Games Teaching.* London: MacDonald and Evans, 1970, p. 77.

Mosston, Muska. *Teaching Physical Education.* Columbus, Ohio: Charles E. Merrill Co., 1966.

Chapter

Games Analysis—
Process Directed

Using the information in the previous chapter, anyone can design a new game or alter an existing game. One simply needs to select from the known game alternative components, provide a structure or form for these components, and the end result is creation of a game.

As the games analysis model suggests, many choices are available to game designers as they create or modify a game. Consequently, game designers must make decisions constantly about the structure of games. The games analysis model is a practical device that will assist game designers with strategies for creating new games. It allows everyone to design games systematically that can accommodate any recreational or educational objective.

THE GAMES ANALYSIS PROCESS

It is necessary at this point to differentiate between the games analysis model and the games analysis process. The *model* is simply a tool that helps people to understand the design of any movement game. It provides us with a common point of departure for examining game design, making it easy to discuss game structure. The *process* is people oriented—it requires that game designers learn how to change from one belief to another. The games analysis process has five steps. Some people complete all five steps in a short time, while others remain at one or more of the steps for an extended period of time.

TABLE 2-1.
COUPLES RACES

Players	Equipment	Movements	Organ. Pattern	Limitations	Purpose
unlimited number of teams, 2 players per team	human bodies	running jumping skipping	2 parallel lines facing one another	Game leader gives one line of players three tasks to perform in sequence: run up to partner, jump over partner, skip back to start position. The race is over when everyone has returned to the starting line.	To enhance auditory memory. To promote locomotor skill practice.

THE FIVE STEPS

The first step involves understanding the games analysis model thoroughly. It is important to understand the language of game categories. The games analysis model was presented in Chapter One, and by this point you should clearly understand the model's language. A good test of whether you do understand the model is to analyze any game or sport by placing the game components in the appropriate game categories (Table 2-1).

The second step requires the game designer to become a risk taker. This is the most difficult step in learning to use the g.a. model, because it requires that you begin to think in terms of alternatives. Using the game analyzed in step one, pick one of the game categories (say, the movement category) and think of all the alternatives which might exist for that category of the game. At this point, the appropriateness of the alternatives you come up with is not important. The trick is to really "brainstorm" and seek many, many alternatives. The author has found that it is often helpful to verbalize, and then commit to paper, the alternatives that come to mind. No idea is incorrect in step two. This step sounds easy, but it is amazing to discover how few alternatives one can deliver during the initial attempt. It has been said that part of creativity is to be able to think in terms of alternatives.

It is very important to understand that some people may at first have difficulty with step two. This may be due, in part, to the notion that there really is only one way to play a game. A person who has grown up with this idea may have a mental block against alternative thinking. Another reason some people have trouble with this step is that their past experience with alternative thinking has been met with less than encouraging support from "significant other" people in their lives. To suggest that alternative thinking in school settings has met with stiff resistance is an understatement. If it is possible to suspend value judgment of the alternatives, then you are on your way to the third step.

Just for fun, Table 2-2 shares some of the alternative movements and equipment suggested by the author's games analysis worhshop participants during the past four years. As you can see, the alternatives are numerous. When given the opportunity, we all can develop at least five alternatives.

Once you begin to feel comfortable thinking in terms of alternatives within one category for one game, shift to another category and repeat the process until you have covered all categories.

TABLE 2-2.
COUPLES RACES

Players	Equipment	Movements	Organ. Pattern	Limitations	Purpose
unlimited number of teams, 2 players per team	human bodies hoops balls jump ropes bean bags balance beams cardboard boxes inner tubes bats milk cartons chairs	run jump skip hop slide gallop leap leap & turn jump & turn crab walk wheelbarrow	2 parallel lines facing one another	Combine any three elements from movements column with appropriate use of elements from equipment column (e.g., see limitations column, Table 2-1).	To enhance auditory memory. To enhance skill development.

Remember that step two is a *thinking* step, without any movement planned. Some people are through with step two in five minutes, while others remain there for quite some time. Again, don't make a value judgment; rather, allow yourself and others time to feel comfortable thinking in alternatives. Once you feel comfortable, move on to step three.

The third step is action oriented. It is now time to try some of the alternatives suggested in step two. Actually try them out. Don't be afraid to succeed or fail. One caution, and it is an obvious one: some alternatives might be unsafe. Earlier it was mentioned that you have to become a risk taker. It is during the third step that this becomes apparent. If you attempt an alternative and it doesn't work, then it is imperative that you continue trying. The easy way out is to quit and say, "I knew it wouldn't work." The opposite of this is to succeed and discover a whole new world of games. That is also a bit scary! Success or failure of your alternative will be measured by the criteria *you* establish. Insofar as possible, try to play the game without judging your alternatives. Try to see the relationship between the performance outcome and the new alternatives you are attempting. This is not easy to do. Judgments should be left for step four.

The fourth step requires you to consider the purpose of the game and decide whether the alternatives you have tried are appropriate. It is now time to make judgments about your newly designed game. If you have allowed yourself to do this prior to step four, you may have limited your ability to think in terms of alternatives. Step four, like step two, is a *thinking* step. Critically examine the performed alternatives in light of the established performance criteria listed in the purpose category. It is assumed that there are identifiable reasons for playing a particular game. Criteria need to be established, but it is not this author's purpose to indicate what is acceptable or unacceptable—that task is left to the individual game designer. An acceptable criterion may be as informal as "I want the children to have fun playing the game" (this can be measured by smiles on their faces or a desire to play the game again and again) or as formal as "I want every child to exhibit a mature catch during every defensive opportunity." The point is that you must determine whether the game performance, as demonstrated by each player, achieved the game purpose. It does seem to be important that games actually do what we say they are going to do. Thus, step four requires cognitive examination of the game alternatives. Repeat this step until you feel comfortable, and then move on to the fifth and final step.

Step five is action oriented. Practice some of the alternatives once again while playing a game, and collect data on the game performance outcome. This can be accomplished by simply observing critically what occurs while the game is being played. You may want to focus your attention only on the kinds of movements the players are making, or you may want to choose another game category to observe critically (e.g., are the organizational patterns appropriate for the desired outcomes?). It is a good idea, initially, to focus your observations on only one category and then expand to others when you feel comfortable. Remember, you are observing the play of individual performers in light of each category's description. For those who want to formalize their data collection, many techniques are available (event recording, duration recording, time sampling, etc.) It is not the intent or scope of this book to present these techniques. If you want to learn about them, look at Siedentop's *Developing Teacher Skills in Physical Education*. Through much practice with step five, you will be able to critically examine, alter, modify, and develop a game to meet the players' needs.

After following this simple process of games analysis, you should feel really comfortable with games. You should feel that you can now analyze and change any movement game. Once you are comfortable with this process, share it with a friend, a fellow games player, and with your students. It is the same process the author has used with elementary, secondary, and adult players. Have fun.

Chapter

The Many Uses
of Games Analysis

Games analysis is process-oriented. It not only provides a model that enables us to analyze any movement game, but it also shares with us how to plan change within a game design. By adjusting game structures in an orderly and sequenced manner, it is possible to enhance the total development of all games players. The suggestion is, of course, that games should be played with specific purposes in mind. If games are to be used in an educational setting for the express purpose of providing specific development opportunities for its participants, then teachers should plan for those experiences by designing games so that these opportunities can be realized. Likewise, recreation leaders may want the games players to experience the joy of play or learn how to interact with a peer and games should be properly designed to accommodate these reasons for game play. Games analysis, as a concept, provides the structure (vehicle) for accomplishing planned change within a games medium.

Games are played for many reasons. This chapter will attempt to demonstrate how games analysis affords the opportunity to all game designers to meet the needs of their performers. There are many uses of games analysis and the following represent just a few.

STUDENT DECISION MAKING VIA
GAMES ANALYSIS

There seems to be an increased sensitivity in our country to return to certain values, such as assuming responsibility for our own actions. This requires that we learn how to make decisions and that consequences exist for each decision we make. If decision making is a necessary survival skill for all of us to possess, and if decision making is a learned process, then it logically seems to follow that an opportunity needs to be provided for us to engage in the decision-making process.

An opportunity to make decisions is given when the teacher allows the youngsters to change the structure of a game to meet the motoric, emotional, and social needs of an individual youngster or a group of youngsters. This is accomplished by allowing the youngsters to change or manipulate one or more of the components within a given category or categories. The youngsters feel that they have some control over their environment. This change in and of itself is often enough to allow many youngsters a feeling of security within the "game world." Moreover, the feeling of security often dramatically enhances performance. Mosston (1966) has written a great deal about the decision-making process within the educational world: "Now, neither teacher nor student can make decisions in a vacuum. Decisions are always made about something. This 'something' is the subject matter of teaching and learning." Mosston certainly saw the teaching-learning act as a shift in decision-making responsibility. Depending on the number and types of decisions, and who made them, certain behaviors would result. If all of the decisions all of the time were made by the teacher, a certain kind of learning would occur. If decision-making responsibility were shifted to the student via an individualization *process* then another kind of learning would occur and a certain type of individual would emerge. Mosston suggests that the shift in decision making to the student produces "the free man whom a free society wishes to produce through its education—education for a society of independent people. Independence implies the ability to make choices among convictions; it connotes the strength to act and pursue the chosen convictions."

It is possible to use the games analysis model as a tool for teaching decision making. Clearly, a spectrum of decision-making opportunity exists:

GAME DESIGN SPECTRUM

Games Leader Designed—Games Leader/Games Player—Games Player

At one end of the spectrum, games leaders make all the decisions all the time regarding game design; whereas at the opposite end of the spectrum, game players make all the decisions all of the time. Thus, the opportunity to engage in game design is variable. It is important to understand that the degree of involvement in game design significantly influences the educational and/or recreational outcome experiences that the game participants enjoy. Games that are totally designed by one individual, introduced to, and played by a group of games players produce experiences for the players that are different from those outcome experiences enjoyed by players who have designed their own game.

A recent study by Marlowe, Fulgozzire, Lerch, and Welch* has demonstrated the influence of game design upon resultant behavioral outcomes experienced by games players. These researchers chose to use the games analysis procedures with emotionally disturbed boys, age 9 to 11. The experimental conditions included: (1) instruction from a teacher in the games analysis process, (2) assessment of each boy's motor skills, and (3) playing vigorous games designed to account for the current stages of motor development by the boys. The purpose of the study was to examine the effectiveness of a therapeutic motor development program based on the games analysis model. They concluded that their motor development program, *based on the games analysis model*, "is effective in reducing feminine game choices of emotionally disturbed boys who are feminine in their play interests."

At the time of this writing, additional research projects are being conducted across the country using the games analysis model and process as a therapeutic device for educational and recreational programs. The exciting prospects for the multiple uses of the model are currently being demonstrated not only by physical educators, but also by special educators and recreational leaders. There are many, many research possibilities using this model. Some possible studies might examine the use of the games analysis process as an instructional and therapeutic aide.

It is important to note that the study by Marlowe et al. addresses the effect decision making has upon gender identification for boys. Certainly one study does not substantiate a proposed

---

*Mike Marlowe et al. "The Games Analysis Intervention as a Method of Decreasing Feminine Play Patterns of Emotionally Disturbed Boys," *Research Quarterly* 49:484-490, December 1978.

hypothesis, but it does lend credibility to much of the field-tested research completed by this author and teachers in and out of this country.

Assuming that one subscribes to the notion that decision making is a learned process *and* that it is a process worth learning, how can games analysis assist with this worthy project? Upon examination of Table 3-1, one can see that it is possible, over a period of time, gradually to relinquish decisions or choices from the games leader to the games participants.

Table 3-1 is simply trying to demonstrate that it is possible to relinquish decisions to games players through the use of the games analysis grid. Field-tested research has indicated that games players should be given only as many choices or decisions as they can handle in a reasonable fashion. Children, in particular, are often provided too many choices at one time and then demonstrate inappropriate behavior. The author suggests that perhaps we "set ourselves up as teachers" for this kind of performance outcome. This need not occur if one would gradually relinquish choices to the players. Every child is different, thus every group of children will respond to the decision-making process differently. It is impossible to indicate how long it will take a group of children to actualize complete freedom of choice. As a matter of fact it may not be your objective, as a games leader, to relinquish all decisions to your players. Table 3-1 does not mean to imply that this should be your objective, rather it simply demonstrates how this might occur. Therefore, this issue does not become a *versus* issue, i.e., game leader-designed games vs. player-designed games. Game designers must only realize that the number and kind of decisions that are relinquished to the game players have a direct effect upon the nature of performance outcomes realized by the players. It is interesting to note what happens socially, emotionally, and intellectually when game design begins to leave the jurisdiction of one person and move to others.

As a teacher or recreation leader you establish a purpose for game play by your students, and depending upon the kind of desired outcomes, you will either allow or not allow them to participate in the design of the game. There are many times that you will want your students to play a game that has already been designed for them. This is perfectly legitimate if the game design accommodates the reason for playing it. It is also legitimate to allow your students to design their own game totally if this is compatible with the expected outcome. Finally, it is possible

TABLE 3-1.
DECISION-MAKING

Game Designed By	Players	Organizational Pattern	Movement	Equipment	Limitations	Purpose
G.L.	G.L.	G.L.	G.L.	G.L.	G.L.	G.L.
G.L.	G.L.	G.L.	G.P.	G.L.	G.L./G.P.	G.L.
G.L./G.P.	G.L./G.P.	G.L.	G.P.	G.P.	G.L./G.P.	G.L.
G.P.	G.P.	G.P.	G.P.	G.P.	G.P.	G.P.

G.L. = game leader makes decision; G.L./G.P. = decisions are shared; G.P. = game players make decisions.

for a games leader/games players to enter the game design spectrum at any place along the spectrum. It is not necessary for games players to begin in games leader-designed games and then move toward games player-designed games. Likewise, it is not necessary for games leaders to feel compelled to move their players along the spectrum. It is most important that games leaders recognize the decision-making ability of their players, understand that a multitude of decision-making alternatives exist, and then act accordingly.

TEACHING TIPS

The author has discovered that some games players seem to make certain decisions about games with more ease than others. It is recommended that games players first be allowed to make decisions about the movement category. Using the new games analysis model, a games leader might want the players to make some decisions about the *type* of movement used in the game. Perhaps a different locomotor or reception/propulsion movement might be suggested. The author has found that it is wise to suggest three alternatives and let the players pick from among the three choices. This strategy immediately lets your students know that it *really* is *o.k.* to change games. You, the games leader, are in effect, sanctioning change. This concept is critical to the success of alternative decision making and yet this initial step is often left out by teachers and recreational leaders. Once children understand that it is permissible to think in terms of alternatives, a new door opens to both of you. As the children become more and more comfortable with this procedure, you should allow them more opportunities to change the components within the movement category. The author has often let children make choices from the quality components and then from the relationship components. Examining the g.a. grid, the order of game choice selection is shown in Table 3-2.

Table 3-2 should be interpreted as a suggested model for allowing games players choices. The model is not absolute and games leaders should feel free to alter the sequence to match their needs. What this model does suggest is that the games analysis grid can provide structure for planned change. The author has found that many games players can make decisions about more than one movement component at one time. It is the responsibility of the teacher or recreation leader to make this final determination.

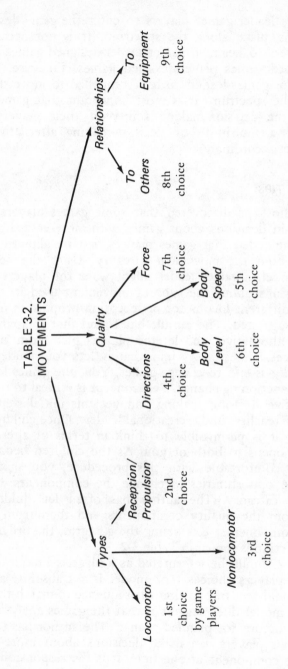

TABLE 3-2.
MOVEMENTS

Relationships
  To Equipment
    9th choice
  To Others
    8th choice

Quality
  Force
    7th choice
  Body Speed
    5th choice
  Body Level
    6th choice
  Directions
    4th choice

Types
  Reception/Propulsion
    2nd choice
  Nonlocomotor
    3rd choice
  Locomotor
    1st choice by game players

The next category from the games analysis model that children seem to feel comfortable making decisions in is the equipment category. This can be followed by allowing the players to make choices in the number of players category or the organizational pattern category.

Experience has shown that, with changes in components in more than one category, it is necessary to adjust the limits category. The following example illustrates this concept:

> Let us assume that a group of sixth graders are playing a game of traditional 5 X 5 basketball employing NCAA basketball rules. It is possible to let the youngsters change a specific movement pattern without having to adjust any of the rules. Let's say they allow only underhand shooting—it is not necessary to adjust any of the stated NCAA rules unless it is felt necessary to sanction non-underhanded shooting.
>
> Now let us say the youngsters change yet another movement component which allows the players to run with the ball. If in addition to this change the youngsters allow seven players/team to be on the court at the same time (player category) and they also add another ball to the game (equipment category), then indeed you must change the limitation category.

Finally, games players should be allowed to make decisions about the limits and purpose categories. Ultimately it is possible that games players are completely designing their own games. Again, some groups of children can accomplish this last thought in a very short time frame, while other groups might never attain this skill.

Children should be allowed to fail when they begin to make decisions. Teachers should be positive in their approach to children who make inappropriate decisions. The fastest way to discourage alternative decision making is to make jest of, or make severe criticism of the children's inappropriate choices.

Identify those decisions that youngsters can handle and build upon them. It is important to teach the students strategies to employ when and if the decision they made was inappropriate. For example, if a group of your students changed the equipment category in the game of baseball so that a golf ball was used as the ball, you need to provide this group of students with a strategy. Within the scope of this situation, it may be appropriate to ask the group first of all to consider the safety of using such a ball in light of the poor visibility the ball would exhibit—someone could get hurt if they couldn't track the ball. Thus you have provided this group of youngsters with an analysis strategy—they must analyze the effect the equipment change may have on the catching performance of the youngsters playing the game. You the teacher can now control the decisions that are made within a game.

> Several years ago I introduced the games analysis concept to a heterogenous group of ninth grade physical education students. It was quite a learning experience for the students as well as for me. After several weeks using the games analysis concept, the students developed one of the most interesting and exciting games that I have ever seen. To begin with, the game was meant to be a softball *type* of game. Part of their assignment was to develop a game that would account for all of the motoric needs of *each* student in the class (38 students). They chose to allow each player to decide what piece of equipment to use when at bat. For example, the highest skilled student chose to use a regulation softball bat and a regulation softball thrown to the batter in the traditional manner. On the other hand, the least skilled student chose to have a large rubber ball rolled toward him and he had to strike the rolling ball with an oversized, underweighted bat. There were many other equipment modifications, but these two examples describe the decision-making extremes. With the equipment changes the students soon learned that there needed to be specific rule changes accompanying the equipment modifications. The resultant game was enthusiastically played by *all* the students because the game structure did not automatically exclude youngsters due to their motor ability. As a matter of fact, the youngsters soon made other changes in their game as they became necessary, and they also seemed to gain a more cooperative spirit within the group. These students reveled in the spirit of decision making relative to physical education class. Slowly but surely they began to understand that individuals were different and that it was all right to possess the physical skills each had at the time.

Rather than suggest a decision-making sequence for the other game categories, the author wants the reader to develop his or her own sequence. If you get stuck, write to Dr. Morris in care of the publisher or simply experiment with the idea of game choice.

One last comment about the use of games analysis as an aid to promote decision making. As decisions about game design shift from the games leader to the games players, creative games are being designed. If you want to engage children in developing creative games, you now have a tool that illustrates how this can be accomplished.

PROBLEM SOLVING VIA GAMES ANALYSIS

Problem solving is considered the highest level of intellectual development. It involves cognition in the identification, analysis, and solution of various problems. There are several kinds of problem-solving behaviors. For example, a problem can be posed to the youngsters which requires them to take apart the whole in order to better understand the parts. Another problem may require putting information together in an orderly manner to gain meaningful understanding of the newly formed whole. Quite another problem may simply be to identify that a problem exists within a given environment. Problems are constantly developing in physical education class and on the play field when youngsters are participating in games. For example, youngsters must constantly deal with analysis of the other team's weaknesses and/or strengths. They must be able to adapt to any change within their play environment so that they successfully cope with it.

Problem solving through games analysis as an approach within physical education requires both physical and cognitive involvement. A major consideration here is that the approach not only can provide opportunities for individuals to seek solutions to stated problems, but, more important, involves the student in the process of asking questions and *defining problems.* It is this unique characteristic of developing and cultivating the ability to independently discover and design new problems which is the essence of this approach.

A child meets daily demands and learns to cope with his environment more effectively through his ability to solve problems using certain logical operations. In this sense children as computers have become more efficient, that is, they are taught to carry out

EXAMPLE OF SOFTBALL-TYPE GAME

logical operations. But is it not equally important that they create problems, seek new possibilities, continually attempt to find a better question *as well as* a better answer for the questions already proposed? The physical education teacher is in an excellent position to provide the type of exhilarating and enthusiastic atmosphere which can foster this growth. Unfortunately, many of those who understand problem solving as a process have "intellect-ualized" themselves out of positions in which they might directly influence children and others. And those who can accomplish the most significant results with problem solving are usually not made aware of its potential and positive nature. Many of us are skeptical of introducing new ideas, not because we wish to maintain the status quo, not because the ideas are radical or difficult to intro-duce, but because the insertion of these different ideas may entail program shifts which in turn might offset more favorable aspects of the existent program.

An important consideration here is the ease with which a problem-solving approach can be included within the already existing physical education activities. When used in a games analysis situation, problem solving can become as integral a part of a program as the teacher feels comfortable with. It can be an exciting aspect of any program and we would be naive to assume that if this is not accepted as an all-or-none commitment, it cannot be made to function effectively. It has merit whether offered as a total program or simply as an addition or augmentation to what already exists.

Before continuing it must be stressed that problem solving as introduced through games analysis is by no means a panacea for the many incongruities which exist between current educational theory and physical education as it is presently practiced in many public schools. It does not pretend to solve all problems nor does it claim to answer all questions. In fact, it may well raise more questions than it answers. But if that is what learning is all about, then this should certainly be a step in the right direction. This approach is not meant to act as a replacement for other important facets of a program. It is a natural part of the learning process which assists the teacher in developing "self moving" individuals who are provided opportunities to search for, analyze, and attempt to solve problems related to game situations within their own range of physical and mental capabilities. It is, therefore, a positive contribution to the fostering of an inquisitive child who can more effectively explore and cope with his environment both physically and mentally.

The implications of such an approach are far-reaching. Everyone can experience success. Incorrect responses are not only never criticized but, in fact, do not even exist; this permits all responses to serve, in some way, as a contribution to the basic learning situation. While not deliberately stressed, other behavioral variables such as self concept, confidence, cooperation among peers begin to emerge as by-products. Each individual is allowed to make decisions based upon self-evaluation, knowledge, skills and attitude; discipline becomes a minor consideration since both physical and mental efforts are constantly being focused on the subject matter.

By relinquishing an increasing number of decisions to the students regarding various aspects of the game situation, the teacher is established as a guide and is not expected to be continually providing correct answers. Much room is left open for creativity on the teacher's part. For example, being able to now pose challenging situations wherein the child can discover numerous problems may add that "extra" amount of excitement lacking in an otherwise adequate program. And finally, the teacher is not required to possess any special amounts of knowledge or high levels of performance ability.

The child who was heretofore labeled as atypical, clumsy or awkward may now be totally included and accepted as an equal since all abilities and all levels of ability are accounted for. Often the child who has the most to gain from games and physical activity programs is also the one who is most easily discouraged by these programs. But now, since all children are given opportunities to make major decisions on questions which were previously decided by others, such children find themselves easily challenged, willing to meet these challenges, and accepted on many more levels than before. The focus is no longer upon accepted standards of movement, but good ideas often become the more important aspect of various situations. Such children are sought for their ability to manipulate game components to accommodate their needs rather than their ability to perform according to predetermined arbitrary standards.

There are several ways to develop problem-solving activities within a games lesson. For many years this has occurred in the areas of gymnastics and dance in the form of movement education. In this approach the activities are less teacher-directed and more student-directed. More and more movement decisions are made by the student for the student rather than by the teacher. A new sense of freedom and responsibility is given to the student. Very few people have attempted to promote independent decision making in a game situation. Kirchner (1974), Maulden and Redfern (1970), and Mosston (1966) have suggested that problem solving and/or freedom to make decisions can also be accomplished in a games situation.

The following are a few specific ideas which you can use to introduce problem solving to your students in grades 3-12. Utilizing the games analysis concept, you provide the students with a game framework which allows the youngsters to meet challenges of the game problem that you initially pose. Allowing youngsters this opportunity to investigate the large realm of solutions and design their game is of inestimable value to their intellectual and social development.

Youngsters in Grades 3-6

Divide the class of youngsters into reasonable working groups, perhaps three to five students per work group. Give each group three balls of various sizes, four hula hoops, and one beanbag. Pose the following problem to them: "Design a throwing, shooting game utilizing all of the equipment—every player must be engaged in the game at all times. In addition develop a rotation system so that everyone on the team gets to perform the game tasks. You have eight minutes to design the game."

With this age group, you need to circulate among all the groups providing necessary direction when it is called for. After a little time has passed, suggest to the groups that they try to play their game without waiting for the other groups to start. Within a very few minutes most of the groups will be performing. Often it is advisable to ask the youngsters to perform their game for the rest of the class. It is surprising how many solutions the youngsters come up with.

Another method of introducing problem solving to youngsters that has worked quite well is to take a game with which they are familiar and ask the whole class for solutions to this problem: "Within the game of prison dodgeball, change the method of moving around the court." Instantly the hands go up—some youngsters will suggest hopping, three-legged movements, skipping—the list is endless.

BASIC CONCEPT—pose a rather simple problem, preferably asking the youngsters to design a game with limited amounts of
equipment, or ask them to change a category within a game they
are familiar with. There are undoubtedly many other methods
which will occur to you. See Table 3-3.

Students in Grades 7-12

Divide the class into teams of five to eight youngsters per
team. Suggest to them that they must create a game utilizing
the equipment you are about to give them. Now you must
prepare equipment boxes prior to class, one box for each
team. Keep the number of individual pieces of equipment the
same for all teams. Some of the following items have been
included in these boxes: bowling pins, jump ropes, lummey
sticks, wands, baseballs, footballs, basketball bladders,
broken bats, and hula hoops. Each team's problem is to
design a game that uses all of the equipment all of the time.
Establish a time frame in which the students must complete
this task. Again, you will be amazed at some of the games
they design. A critical role you, the teacher, must play is to
make sure that they consider safety factors in the use of all
equipment.

Another method that has been used with this age group is
the following: Having introduced the games analysis categories via discussion and visual description, make up a
number of components for each category. Put the components into a hat (by category). Then ask each team (usually
four to five teams of eight players) to send a representative
up to pull four components out of the hat. After this is done
for each category, each team's problem is to design a game
using only the components drawn from the hat.

An example of the above procedure: Put into a hat
movement components such as running, skipping, hopping,
throwing. Each team picks the number of components
specified and then designs a game. The most creative game
receives some kind of reward. This method can be varied in
many ways. For example, you can establish all the components for all of the categories but one. The students pick
components from the hat for just that one category and must
design a game using the given category components and the
"picked-out-of-the-hat" components. One can increase the
degree of difficulty of this problem-solving method by finally

TABLE 3-3.
PROBLEM-SOLVING

Players	Equipment	Movements	Organ. Pattern	Limitations	Purpose
5-8 per team or group	Each group receives a box of equipment—the equipment is different for each box. The following items are included: Ropes Sticks Cardboard cartons Plastic milk cartons Basketball bladders Bats Hoops	Game designers make decisions regarding: type of movement, quality of movement, and relationship of movement.	Game designers make decisions regarding: type of patterns, location of patterns, and position of the team relative to one another and to the equipment.	1. All the equipment must be used all of the time. 2. Game designers make all of the rest of the decisions including: other physical limits, game conditions, game procedures.	Promote convergent problem-solving skills.

having the students pick all of the components for all of the categories. This, therefore, indicates a process is occurring within this problem-solving method. Again, the ability of the students to design these new games will surprise you. Indeed, the interest in physical education at the high school level seems to increase with the promotion of game design via problem solving. Each youngster now begins to share in the process of making a new game or a variation of one already known. Do you think that finding answers to problems that arise in designing a game and playing it with mutual consent is of value to students? Perhaps it is of more value to design your own game than to learn prestructured games with externally imposed rules year after year. You may discover more about your students as individual human beings than you ever thought possible.

A final method of introducing problem solving for this age group is to get the students to consider the feelings and capabilities of others. Pose this problem: "Design a striking game (using given equipment) that mandates everyone is involved at the same time yet within the movement task each individual can choose how he wants the object delivered and each individual can have his choice of striking implement and size of object being struck." This is a more complicated problem that may require more guidance from you the teacher as well as more time in which to solve it. The reaction of many youngsters of various ages to this kind of problem has shown that they are forced to think about and account for other students' feelings and capabilities. It does require thinking and experimenting time—give it to them. Experience also shows that it is helpful to require the students to write out the game in a grid, accompanying the grid with a description of how to play the game. This suggests that the students bring pencils and paper to class—granted, an un-heard-of behavior.

Certainly this last section utilizing problem solving implies that youngsters should be allowed to design creative games. It is through creative game design that students from grades 3 to 12 begin to understand the relationships among categories within a game structure. The students, at all grade levels, soon realize why it is necessary to have rules, how a change in one category affects the design of another category, how within a game there is a place for everyone's abilities, and, most importantly, how differences in ability make one feel good or bad about oneself. Kirchner (1974) suggests that youngsters in grades 3-6 be given initial problems guiding the movement tasks via a movement theme approach. The following is an attempt to summarize the kinds of experiences the teacher might consider in asking youngsters to create games.*

Level 1, Age 8-9—Youngsters seem interested in participating on a group team whose objective is to beat another team—youngsters are still interested in enhancing their own individual skills—youngsters are interested in older children's games but accept readily modified versions— visual perceptual apparatus permits horizontal and vertical tracking of objects—movement control is satisfactory but they still may have difficulty in movement reactions to various movement situations. These youngsters are just learning to abide by rules and accept the judgment of others relative to rule attention.

Level 2, Age 10-12—Youngsters more interested in team play—they are able to concern themselves with the group (team) outcome; it is important that the "team" win—they more readily accept a code of rules governing the methods of play—additionally they exhibit a readiness to abide by subjective interpretations of the rules by other players or an external referee—the visual tracking apparatus is generally mature allowing for complex tracking capabilities. Movement control of body parts and the total body is much improved. They better react to changing game situations in movement sense. Physically they are stronger and consequently can perform more difficult movement tasks. They can understand inner workings of a game structure.

*Adapted from *Games Teaching* by E. Mauldon and H. B. Redfern (London: MacDonald and Evans, 1970).

Level 3, Age 13-14—Youngsters are capable of abiding by rules—they are also capable of understanding the structure of a game—this is the time to work on developing emotional and social growth within a game—due to puberty some movement capabilities are improved or altered; realize the effect this has upon their self concept within a game—they are concerned with precise rules, strategies, and tactics.

Level 4, Age 15-17—Students are capable of understanding emotions of others—they also want to exhibit precise skills within a game concept but they are most willing to perform problem-solving activities within a game—highly creative if given the chance.

The preceding information is by no means complete. It is an attempt to summarize the necessary considerations teachers must realize when they design learning situations during a games lesson in physical education. Notice third grade is the lowest grade at which it is suggested you employ the games analysis concept. Jean Piaget suggests forcing youngsters at too early an age into competitive situations may prove most damaging to their developing stages of understanding the nature and function of rules. Remember that not all youngsters develop at the same rate; that is why it is important to learn how to change the games children play.

Now that the reader is familiar with the games analysis model, and is beginning to understand how the model can be used, it is only necessary to indicate that one can design either convergent problems or divergent problems for their games players. The new model should make it easier for the games leader to present these kinds of problems to the games players.

NEW GAMES FROM OLD

It has been suggested previously that teachers and students alike can design new games from existing traditional games. There are many reasons why one would want to do just this. You may want to design another game that approximates the traditional game so that the youngsters can develop certain skills. For example, you want to introduce your class to the traditional game of volleyball because you are interested in the game and because you believe that the game will help develop good hand-eye coordination. You work for a few days on some of the basic skills and feel that the youngsters are now ready for a game. Unfortunately, after five minutes of play the students become bored and start to hit the ball everywhere except where it should be going. Some of the students seemingly could care less if the ball came within a foot of them; they are becoming very restless. What should you do? Again, the first thing is to analyze your game. Can each student perform the basic skills involved? If the answer is no, what factors are the cause? Could the equipment being used possibly be a limiting factor? Instead of using a traditional leather ball, try a plastic ball (often found at large displays in grocery stores). Often just the change in the equipment being used is enough to promote game success, particularly with younger students.

Let's continue with our volleyball game for a moment more. Suppose you have introduced the game to a group of fifth and sixth grade youngsters—this is the first time they have played the game. You also want to teach them the traditional game of volleyball, but after three minutes you realize that the game is not going just as you planned. The students are missing the ball, they are consistently hitting the ball into the net as well as hitting the ball four or five times on one side. What should you do?

Again, look at the game in terms of the skills necessary to play the game. Are the students able to perform the skills? Let's assume in this instance that they can each individually perform the skills but when they are asked to perform in this group setting something happens. What, if anything, seems to affect their ability to get the ball over the net? Could it be the equipment? If yes, change the ball or adjust the net height off the ground. Teachers often set the net at arm's length height, only to produce frustration on the part of the students. Now let's assume that the youngsters can begin to get the ball over the net with some degree of regularity but many are still having difficulty returning the ball after they hit it once. It is suggested that you, the teacher, mandate a rule change. Allow the youngsters to hit the ball three, four, or five times if they need to gain control over the ball before returning the ball to the net. If our goal is to get youngsters interested in a game let's not deprive them of the enjoyment of succeeding before they develop all of the necessary motor skills. It just may be that many youngsters need the extra time of the "additional" hits to gain control over the ball before returning the ball to the other side. We in physical education should strive for

motoric control of our body parts rather than seek quantity results (how far, how fast). By allowing a slight rule change in the traditional game of volleyball you have provided the students with new hopes for success.

If you don't want to call these "new" games by their traditional name, make up your own names. If a game does not promote the reaction that you expected, take a moment to analyze why. The beginning teacher utilizing the games analysis concept may want to write out the traditional game in a grid. Then by inspection of several of the categories you can begin to find solutions from re-playing the game. You have now developed "new" games from the "old" games. See Chapter 6 for additional game designs of specific sports.

LEAD-UP GAMES DEVELOPING
SPECIFIC MOTOR SKILLS

As physical educators we are aware of the fact that we should provide games that lead into the traditional or terminal game. We call these games lead-ups. If we are going to teach the students the game of football, we should not expect them to be able to play the game of football efficiently on the very first day. Rather we develop over a period of days and/or weeks the skills necessary to play the game. Thus we play lead-up games that require the use of these developing skills. In this way we gradually introduce the students to the skills and concepts of football. Games analysis can help the teacher program the development of the motor skills and game concepts necessary for participation in the game. How? Each teacher has individual preferences in teaching sports skills. It is not the purpose here to suggest what these skill progressions should or should not be. Rather the intention is to demonstrate how a teacher can use the games analysis concept via utilization of the grid to help plan, over a period of time, specific lead-up games terminating in the final game objective.

First, decide on the terminal game objective in terms of skill requirement and concept involvement. Basically you are writing behavioral objectives for the day's lesson. Write this game in the grid. Next, plan how and when you will teach specific motor skills and game concepts. Let's assume that a typical teaching session allows for warm-up activities, followed by introduction and practice of the skills to be learned that day. Finally, you may decide to end the day's session with some kind of game activity (relay or lead-up game). Of course, this regimen will not be followed each day, as no two teachers follow exactly the same pattern of skill teaching. Let's see now how one can develop some lead-up games. The example used will be football at the sixth grade level. Notice the stated behavioral objectives relative to psycho-motor development (motor) and cognitive development (concepts). Each objective can be observed and measured.

UNIT—Football Skills and Concepts
OBJECTIVES—Motor:
  Develop ability to pass the football a distance of 10 yards with accuracy; hand the ball off without fumbling the ball; center the ball with accuracy a distance of 5 feet; punt the football with accuracy a distance of 15 yards; catch a thrown

football at 10 feet, 5 of 10 attempts, display ability to run with the ball; demonstrate ability to screen block.
OBJECTIVES—Concepts:
Students will understand via performance the following concepts: line of scrimmage, scoring system, five running plays, five pass patterns, rules of touch football, defensive positioning, offensive positioning.

Then, using your own procedures, begin to teach the motor skills and combine these same skills with the aforementioned game concepts. Try to combine several of the motor skills and/or concepts into some form of game to promote interest or move toward the terminal game objective—regulation touch football.

Games analysis can be most helpful at this point for both the new and the experienced teacher. You can design new games or alter existing games to meet the needs of your students. One can find countless lead-up games that purport to promote certain motor skills development, but how many times have you found that these suggested games don't quite fit your situation? Simply adjust these games via the games analysis grid.

Let us now look at a very limited number of games designed via the games analysis approach (Table 3-4).

Now let's assume that something goes wrong with this particular game. For instance, the distance between players is causing the center pass to be bounced to the receiver. Simply shorten the distance between players. This sounds like a simple-minded answer that all of us know, but we have all known teachers who would not change anything in the game because "then one isn't playing the game the way it was meant to be played." Are we in physical education more interested in the outcome or in the process of skill development for all youngsters?

Let's carry the center pass relay one more step. Assume that even when the players are moved closer together many of them are still dropping the ball. Change the organizational pattern. Rather than having each team side by side, split the teams into the various geographical parts of the field or stagger the columns—both suggestions are shown on p. 54.

TABLE 3-4.
CENTER PASS RELAY

Name of Game	Players	Equipment	Movement Pattern	Organizational Pattern	Limitations	Purpose
1. Center Pass Relay	5 - ? team	1 ball per team	Center pass, running	Each team is in column formation 5 ft. from one another.	The players must stay 5 ft. from one another. The ball is centered from the first player to the next player. This continues until the last player receives the ball. He then runs to front of line, line moves back one player. First team to return to original start position is the winner.	1. To develop center pass skill. To promote team cooperation. To combine center pass with running the ball.

```
X   X X X X   X              X

X             X              X X

X             X      or      X X X

X   X X X X   X              X X X X

                              X X X

                              X X

                              X
```

Can you think of other organizational patterns? What does changing the organizational patterns do for the game? One thing it might do is begin to focus the attention upon each person's own team performance rather than worrying how well the other teams are doing. There are many alternatives to reduce team tension—can you think of some other changes? THERE IS MORE THAN ONE WAY TO PLAY A GAME.

So far we have looked at adjustment of one game designed to promote skill development of the center pass and running with the ball after it has been received. The following games show how a teacher can design even more games as lead-ups to the terminal objective.

By changing the type of movement allowed in a game you have designed another game to fit the needs of the game purpose. Again, this concept is not unique, but it should point out to the teacher how one can develop a number of games from perhaps just one original game. It has been found advantageous to begin designing games by first describing the purpose of the game, then complete the other categories to meet the students' needs. With some practice a creative teacher can quite easily design lead-up games for almost any situation. The more a teacher performs this task the easier it becomes.

Finally, the type of game designed needs to reflect current growth and development information and current motor learning theory. It is not the purpose of this book to present a great wealth of growth and development information and then demonstrate how this information influences motor development. You will be shown how to use the games analysis grid to account for the various stages youngsters in elementary school go through. We will then deal primarily with visual perception as a developmental process.

TABLE 3-5.
SIX-MAN SCORE

Name of Game	Players	Equipment	Movement	Organ. Patterns	Limitations	Purpose
1. Six-Man Score	6/team	1 ball/team	running handoffs blocking	Each team's decision within limits described	Must have one center, one Q.B., one back, other three players you must position anywhere behind line of scrimmage. Only screen blocking allowed. May only use one play twice in succession, must use all five running plays you've designed. You have 8 plays to score a T.D. Field is 30-40 yds. long. Defensive 6 players must tag with 2 hands below the shoulders. Offsides not allowed, replay if this occurs. Six points for T.D., 3 points if defense prevents T.D. Game is over after each team of 6 has been on offense 3 times.	To develop 5 running plays. To learn initial rules of line of scrimmage, offsides, two hand touch. To develop team play. To develop offensive and defensive concepts.
2. Six-Man Score w/Pass	same as above	same as above	running catching passing	same as above	Same limits as above but this time you can only pass the ball. Defense must count to 5 before rushing the passer. If defense intercepts they may try to score on same play 6 pts. 1 point for each incomplete pass for defensive team.	Same as above with these additions: To develop pass plays, to develop offensive and defensive strategies vs. pass.

When youngsters enter the first grade they possess an ability to track horizontally moving targets much more effectively than vertically moving objects. Therefore in primary grades, K-2, any game that requires visual tracking should be designed so that the performer only has to track on the horizontal plane. The next developmental stage, usually around grades 2-3, allows the youngsters to process information efficiently from vertically moving objects. Thus any game that now involves tracking could incorporate horizontal and vertical tracking. The ability to track a three-dimensional object through a variety of planes does not seem to appear until late grade 2 or grade 3. In addition, the ability to track an object through a variety of planes and move oneself to intercept the object does not seem to appear until grades 3-4. This is the reason why so many T-ball baseball players fail to catch a ball after running after a fly ball. This visual-perceptual information must be accounted for in the design of games that require tracking an object. The visual development of youngsters involves a process—a process implies moving from one condition to another. The age at which they go through this process is not the same for all youngsters. Some youngsters' visual-perceptual processes are quite mature at eight years of age while in others these processes mature much later. The fact that youngsters do not all develop at the same rate has dramatic implications for success in motor performance if a game is so structured that it does not consider the stage of development each youngster has reached. Certainly any game requiring visual tracking needs to account for the several developmental stages that each class of youngsters will exhibit. This is one reason for not playing too many team games with youngsters below grade 3. By the time grade 3 is reached many of the school age children are better able to handle game situations physically, emotionally, and socially.

According to Piaget (1965), Sutton-Smith (1971), and Loy and Inghan (1973), youngsters' ability to handle situations emotionally and socially also undergoes a developmental process. Helanko (1957) developed a table of socialization stages. For example, youngsters age 5-6 regard rules as sacred and absolute. These same youngsters exhibit a great deal of egocentric behavior. Thus to try to teach team games to this age group is most difficult, though possible. It is more important for this age group to experience a wealth of movement experiences. By ages 7-9, youngsters begin to exhibit cooperative behavior, and games rules need not be absolute. By the ages of 10-12 youngsters are capable of handling complex social interactions involving cooperation and competition. Rules are regarded as relative and solid group identities are being formed. Any game designed for middle and upper elementary school can begin to build into itself situations that promote cooperative behavior. Concurrently this is the age to deal with emotional and social reactions and conflicts that develop due to game design.

As mentioned in an earlier chapter, the game design may predispose itself to certain emotional and social conflicts. You, the teacher, must recognize what in a game is causing the inappropriate behavior. Is the game design too complex to allow for proper comprehension of the rules? Take the following example:

> I had a group of fourth and fifth graders who loved to play a rather complicated game of dodgeball. By design the game required subjective judgment on the part of the person throwing the ball as well as by the person getting hit by the ball. There was so much arguing and physical fighting that I had to stop the game. The youngsters were not able to "live up to the rules" and/or some honestly had no idea what the rules were. Changing a rule or two and focusing attention on the desired social and emotional behavior resulted in appropriate interaction. The process took four weeks.

This is a classic example of game design influencing social and emotional growth. As a teacher, you must recognize that too many rules within a game or too many components within any of the categories can lead to confusion on the part of the players. In asking a youngster to remember the structure of any given game you are assuming the possession of a most efficient short- and long-term auditory and visual memory. A limiting factor in poor gamesmanship on the part of the players is their failure to remember what they were supposed to do. Therefore, have each game build upon the previous one in terms of tasks one has to do and remember. Another cause for social sanctioning occurring in a game is subjective evaluation of rules by the participants. For example, youngsters called upon to evaluate subjectively whether or not they were tagged with two hands below the waist might lie about the results, depending on age and/or the major game outcome. If you haven't dealt with group interaction behavior, then don't design a tournament where the top team receives some kind of reward. If you do, you are implying to the youngsters indirectly, by design, that the most important thing is to win rather than to understand the process of playing a game. A game purpose can be stated: learn how to cooperate, learn how rules affect group behavior, learn how to abide by the rules. Games designed to fulfill this purpose have been tried with fifth and sixth graders with resounding success. The following is an example:

> A class of 35 fifth and sixth graders was given the objective of displaying (1) knowledge of the rules; (2) acceptance of subjective interpretation of the rules by opposing team members; (3) strategies to deal with opposing rule interpretations. Prior to playing a complex game of dodgeball, the entire class was taught how to display the three behavioral objectives mentioned. The game of dodgeball was designed so that the purpose of the game was to win by displaying the three desired behaviors.
>
> Using a wrist counter, I viewed the game and kept "score" by counting each desired behavior when it occurred and recording it on a score sheet. After the game, we talked about the significance of the score. Having done this for several days, a student finally said, "Mr. Morris, it's not important what the score is cuz it's more fun to play the game without arguing—that's what we're learning, huh?"

The teacher's major role, then, is to examine the structure of the game and ascertain whether the structure is too complex to be internalized. If the youngsters can't make appropriate subjective interpretation of the rules, don't design a game which mandates that this occur. In the case of the touch football game, simply design the game so that the defense has to pull a flag off—this is objective and easily evaluated. Youngsters from grades 4-12 can learn how complex games can become. They can learn the relationship one category within a game has upon another category, and they can learn why rules are important. Often "cheating" in a game at the elementary school level is nothing more than forgetting a rule or never really understanding what the rule was in the first place. Have you had this occur?

Mike says, "Mr. Morris, John was cheating cuz he started before he was tagged!" Here's a solution to this problem—ask Mike to explain the rule to John. Focus the attention on Mike's explanation of the rule to John. What you are doing indirectly and very subtly is providing the class with a strategy to employ if they think someone is "cheating." The strategy is to reinforce the rule. If John chooses to break the rule the next time he plays the game, then say to him, "John, you indicated to me that you know the rule. Can I help you understand it? No? Well then, show me you know the rule."

More often than not John will no longer "cheat." If, however, he does break the rule, employ this strategy: "John, you have a choice to make—you may play the game demonstrating you know the rule or you can play the game and break the rule and then you get to sit out of the remaining games." John will now usually abide by the rule—if he doesn't, you must follow through by saying, "John, I see *you* have decided to sit out." This way John accepts the responsibility for his behavior.

What is suggested here is that as a teacher you initially reinforce the rule, then reinforce the desired outcome because the youngsters may simply need to be re-cued as their auditory or visual memory may not have been functioning adequately. Finally, give the youngsters realistic choices so that they have control over the play environment. This is one method to teach responsibility within a games lesson. Remember, one of our rules as educators is to help the child develop as a total human being, and much can be learned within a games environment.

INCLUSION RATHER THAN EXCLUSION

P. L. 94-142 has been in effect since September 1, 1978. To the maximum extent possible, all handicapped students are to be placed within a mainstream setting if it is the least restrictive environment for the child. Games analysis can assist with this process of including handicapped children. Game activities can be designed to directly accommodate the movement ability of any child. *HOW?*

First, the games leader needs to subscribe to the notion that there is more than one way to play a game. Additionally, one needs to believe that within a single game design, the players can be involved in different movements at the same time. The following is an example:

The game is kickball. A highly skilled player should be expected to kick a soccer ball that is pitched at a high rate of speed. A lesser skilled player (regardless of causative reason, e.g., mental retardation, minimal brain dysfunction, cerebral palsy) should be allowed to kick a larger ball that is stationary.

The inclusion of all children is directly related to attitude and game design. If you can accept the preceding example, then you are on your way to including all children.

Within a single game design it is imperative that games leaders match the game tasks (requirements) with the developmental status of each child. One way this author has accomplished this is to use the games analysis grid as an assessment tool. The following scenario represents a typical educational setting the author has found himself in during the past three years. Here is how he used games analysis to aid the realization of the inclusion concept:

"While playing softball with my class of sixth graders, it came to pass that four 'handicapped' children were mainstreamed into the class. Their movement abilities ranged from immature throwing patterns to immature striking patterns. Realizing that these children possessed some movement abilities equal to and less than the other children's abilities, I quickly realized that I needed to really know what kinds of movements all of my students could perform. Therefore I chose to use just the movement category from the model as I observed them play a game. Using appropriate observation assessment techniques I discovered that most of the children could perform the locomotor tasks fairly well. Although most of them had little difficulty with their nonlocomotor movements, many of the children exhibited immature propulsion and reception skills. This was particularly true when certain qualities of movement were witnessed. For example, when the children were asked to move *backwards* to catch a ball traveling at a *fast* rate of speed they seemed to drop it. Thus I found that the g.a. model forced me to focus on several very specific components of movement, allowing me to assess the abilities of my students. I discovered that several children could hit a large ball when it was stationary but could not strike a moving ball. Some children had more success using a larger bat (circumference) while other children met success with a smaller bat. Reason suggested that I structure a game that permitted players to choose from a variety of equipment alternatives and allow the players to strike at either a moving or stationary ball. It worked!!''

What occurred in the preceding story was that the teacher matched the striking task with the ability of the child, thus including the child rather than excluding him or her.

Many teachers have also discovered other ways of including all children. Here's one method that seems to work well. Regardless of the game, establish movement tasks that accommodate the full spectrum of the motor abilities in your class and allow any of the players at any time to engage in any task. An example of this idea follows:

BASKETBALL GAME SPECTRUM

Skill Continuum:	Less Skilled ◄——► More Skilled	
Specific Skill:	Can shoot a ball through a vertical hoop 7 ft. off the ground	Can shoot a ball through a horizontal hoop (regular backboard) 10 ft. off the ground

Within the game make it possible to score points when shooting at a 7-foot-high basket (vertical basket) and when shooting at a 10-foot-high basket (regular backboard). Notice that you are now "sanctioning" individual differences by demonstrating an acceptable behavior for each child's motor ability. Also notice that no particular mention was made of the handicapping condition. Rather, the focus is upon the overt motor performance—what the child can do. Once you know what the children can do, then simply design several tasks that accommodate their ability. Allow any child to perform any of the tasks. If you are concerned that the more highly skilled children will choose the "easier tasks," attach more points to the "more difficult" tasks. In this manner everyone can feel that they are contributing to the team.

It is imperative that we look at children's motor ability or motor status rather than look upon children as being "handicapped" or functioning at a "normal" level. If we can look at motor ability and design tasks in a game that accommodate the various abilities, then we will be including all children in games. Another method of including handicapped children is to teach them compensatory skills, work with them to master these skills, and include them in games that are in no way altered.

Finally, ask the children to design activities that incorporate all skill levels. The children come up with the best answers. All one has to do is visit any sand lot or neighborhood playground and watch the children of all sizes, ages, and abilities engage in team games. The children make all sorts of adjustments in game designs in order to allow every child to have *an equal opportunity to succeed and fail*. Here are two real examples:

Neighborhood basketball game:

Four children playing on a neighbor's driveway basketball court. Two of the children were 6 to 8 inches taller than their younger opponents. To "equalize" the game, they changed the traditional basketball rules. The older boys had to bring the ball back out to a line on the pavement after every exchange of ball possession, whereas the younger players did not. The younger players could put up a shot after every rebound. The older boys also had to shoot the ball from a minimum of 8 feet from the basket, enabling the younger, shorter players a chance at rebounding the ball.

Neighborhood pick up baseball game:

Eight children were playing, aged 6 years to 14 years. The two teams were equally divided with young and old players. The rules stated that whenever a younger player came to bat, he or she would hit a stationary ball placed on a batting tee, while the older players had to hit a thrown ball. The acceptable boundaries for a base hit were larger for the younger children than for the older children.

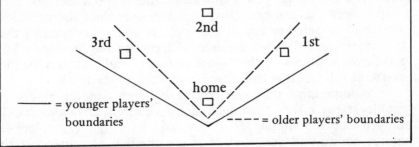

I often think that sometimes we are much better off to let the children design their own games rather than impose our game designs on them. The children can be incredibly clever, wise, and resourceful . . . if we would only let them.

It is possible to include rather than exclude. For more information on this concept, read *Elementary Physical Education—Toward Inclusion**, because much more detail about this concept is presented in this book.

ADAPTING THE NEW GAMES

Since the first edition of this games book was published, a wonderful book entitled *The New Games Book*** has been placed on the market. The games include modifications of older games and many newly designed games as well. If you haven't read this book, please do. This author has been altering or modifying many of the new games, using the games analysis process. Table 3-6 illustrates Hunker Hawser (a New Game) and a modification of it. The change occurred primarily in the categories of organizational pattern and movement, with minor adjustments in the limitations category. By using the g.a. model, the author simply listed several alternatives for each category. The more you employ this technique, the easier it becomes to develop your own games.

SEQUENCING SKILL DEVELOP-
MENT THROUGH GAMES

The author has indicated earlier in this chapter that it is possible to include any number of skill abilities within a single game form if you structure the game appropriately. It is also possible to present games sequentially in a specific order that enables each successive game to increase in difficulty.

If games are to be designed that permit the players to develop motor skill, the design must provide opportunities for the players to practice the skill. Motor learning principles indicate that quality practice time must be sufficient if an individual is to master a motor task. It is possible to design games that permit all children to have such opportunities.

---

*G. S. Don Morris, *Elementary Physical Education—Toward Inclusion* (Salt Lake City: Brighton Publishing Company, 1980).
**Andrew Fluegelman, ed., *The New Games Book* (Garden City, N.Y.: Dolphin Books, Doubleday and Company, 1976).

TABLE 3-6.
HAWSER

	Players	Equipment	Movement Pattern	Organizational Pattern	Limitations	Purpose
Hunker Hawser	2	1 rope per 2 players 1 stump per player	tugging on rope, balancing on stump	Players facing one another	Both players must stay on their own stump. When you pull the other player off his/her stump, winner is declared.	pull the player off the stump by tugging on a rope held by both players.
Back to Back Hawser	same as above	same as above	same as above	Version 1: players' backs to one another but they still hold the rope between them.	same as above	same as above
			one-foot balance	Version 2: players face one another but may only balance on one foot on their stump.	same as above or winner is declared if either player touches nonsupport foot to the stump or ground	

Before proceeding further, the author should like to indicate that there are more efficient teaching strategies that should be used when teaching movement skills to players. For example, it may be more efficient to use learning centers to teach children locomotor, reception, or propulsion skills. It may be more appropriate for some children to learn movement skills using different media. Game forms, however, can be used as another means to allow the skills to be practiced. The games analysis process assists the teacher in accommodating the spectrum of skill levels found in all classes. More information is presented in the next chapter regarding the development of game skills.

A games analysis grid can assist with the sequential presentation of movement tasks from one game to the next. Table 3-7 provides the schema.

The idea is, as you can see, most simple. It does presuppose that game designers and leaders know how to increase the degree of difficulty of motor tasks. One way of increasing the degree of difficulty of motor tasks is to factor analyze each motor task. For example, in the game analyzed in Table 3-7, the factor of distance was involved in making the bowling task more difficult. By increasing the distance the bowler is from the bowling pins, you make the task more difficult. Likewise, it is possible to increase the number of times a child has to jump the rope or it is possible to increase the height of the rope the child must jump. Finally, it is possible to increase the height of the basket a child attempts to shoot at. In game one you could have the players shoot at a 7-foot-high basket, in game two have them shoot at a 10-foot-high basket with a hula hoop hanging from the rim, and in game three have the players shoot at just the 10-foot-high basket. In this manner you have increased the difficulty of the task. Remember this is only an example of another use of games analysis. You, the games leader, must design the games to meet your players' needs. It is beyond the scope of this book to provide a comprehensive discussion of this idea and the concept application of a factor analysis. For a much more detailed presentation of these ideas, see the book entitled *Elementary Physical Education— Toward Inclusion**

Given that a full range of skill abilities exists within any one group of children and given that these same children bring to the game's experience a large spectrum of needs and interests, it is

*Morris, G. S. Don, *Elementary Physical Education—Toward Inclusion* (Salt Lake City: Brighton Publishing Company, 1980).

BACK-TO-BACK HAWSER

TABLE 3-7.
SEQUENCING MOTOR TASKS ACROSS SEVERAL GAMES

Game Sequence	Players	Equipment	Movement Pattern	Organizational Pattern	Limitations	Purpose	Degree of Difficulty
Game 1	30 children. 6 teams of 5 players.	milk cartons, 2 balls per team, 1 jump rope per team, basketball targets	bowl over the cartons, jump the rope, shoot the balls into the basketball target	column relay formation	1. 1 bowling opportunity per player. 2. Jump the rope 5 times. 3. 1 opportunity for basket shooting. 4. You make up the other rules.	To enable all players to practice bowling, rope jumping, and basketball shooting practice.	simple or easy
Game 2	same as above	same as above but add more equipment	Increase D of D* of bowling. Increase D of D for rope jumping. Increase D of D for basket shooting.	same as above	same as above with any necessary changes	same as above	increased difficulty

*D of D = degree of difficulty.

TABLE 3-7 (Continued)

Game 3	same as above	same as above but add more equipment	Increase D of D for all three motor tasks.	same as above	same as above with any necessary changes	same as above	greater difficulty and/or most complex

*D of D = degree of difficulty.

encumbent upon game designers to develop game situations that begin to include all children. By this point in the book, you should understand that the author has shared many game design strategies with you that enable a larger spectrum of performance levels displayed by children to indeed be included within singular game forms. Games analysis allows you to design a game any way you need to in order to accommodate all children. Games analysis really is sanctioning the notion that it is o.k. to be different, perform at different levels and possess unique, individual needs. Hopefully, by providing this acceptance sanction and by providing strategies to allow a game designer to include all children, a truly humanistic attitude might prevail within a games environment.

References

Helanko, R. pp. 238-47 of *Personality and Social Systems,* ed. N.J. Smelser and W. T. Smelser. New York: Wiley, 1963 [article reprinted from *Acta Sociologica* 2 (1957): 229-40].

Kirchner, Glenn. *Physical Education for Elementary School Children,* 4th Ed., Dubuque, Iowa: William C. Brown Co., 1979.

Loy, J.W., and Inghan, Alan G. "Play, Games and Sport in the Psychosocial Development of Children and Youth," pp. 257-306 in *Physical Activity,* ed. Lawrence Rarich. New York: Academic Press, 1973.

Loy, J.W., and Kenyon, G.S., eds. *Sports Culture and Society.* Englewood Cliffs, N.J.: Prentice-Hall, 1959.

Mauldon, E., and Redfern, H.B. *Games Teaching.* London: MacDonald and Evans, 1970.

Mosston, Muska. *Teaching Physical Education.* Columbus, Ohio: Charles E. Merrill Co., 1966.

Piaget, Jean. *The Moral Judgement of the Child.* New York: Free Press, 1965.

Sutton Smith, B. Paper delivered at 2nd World Symposium of Historical Sport and Physical Education, Banff, Alberta, Canada, 1971. Reprinted in *Physical Activity,* ed. Lawrence Rarich. New York: Academic Press, 1973.

Sutton-Smith, B., and Rosenberg, B.G. pp. 280-82 of *Physical Activity,* ed. Lawrence Rarich. New York: Academic Press, 1973 [article reprinted from *Journal of American Folklore* 74 (1961): 17-46].

Chapter

Would You Like to Have Skillful Games Players?

The playing of games requires that the players be able to make motor adjustments as they interact with other players, game conditions, and game equipment. How many times have you, as a games teacher, working with your players on very specific game skills (e.g., basketball dribbling), observed that most of the players developed the skill well, only to have it rapidly deteriorate during the game? Many, many teachers all over the United States have shared this common experience with this author. The reason this occurs is that the players "learned" to perform the skill under one set of performance conditions (standing still while dribbling, then dribbling the ball about a prescribed area) and then the players were asked to perform the same kind of skill under another set of conditions (in a competitive game setting with defensive players). The traditional or typical method of teaching game skills does not often lend itself to accommodate the notion that a multitude of game conditions influence individual game skill performances. It is not true that game skills are necessarily always predictable. You see, during a basketball game the players must dribble a ball while moving in different *directions*, at different *speeds*, while maintaining different body *levels* and *shapes*. Thus, game players must experience a host of gamelike conditions if they are truly to be efficient during the playing of a game.

This author suggests that becoming efficient in games play really involves a four-step process. Another excellent book available to game leaders is *Physical Education For Children: A Focus*

71

*on the Teaching Process.** Of special interest to games teachers is the section written by Kate Barrett that presents a similar process.

THE PROCESS

This author suggests that a four-step process is involved in developing efficient, effective, and skillful games players. The first step requires that games teachers analyze a game, determine what the individual skills are, and then have the players develop each skill to a particular competency level. For example, the game of basketball is composed of these skills: dribbling, passing, shooting, running, jumping, dodging, guarding, and many more. The games teacher needs to critically analyze the motor composition of the game and then design instructional settings that enable the players to practice the skills. Once a particular "mastery" competency level has been reached it is possible to move to the next step.

This second step is crucial—it involves designing gamelike instructional settings that allow the players to practice their newly acquired skills in conditions that approximate actual game conditions. For example, let's assume that during the teaching of basketball to a group of individuals, the teacher has identified that the players need work on dribbling the ball while moving in relation to other players, equipment, and prescribed boundaries. Involvement in a gamelike setting mandates that the players "learn" how to make the bodily adjustments necessary for successful participation in this activity. The following gamelike activity is characteristic of this concept as it relates to the preceding situation.

Game teachers can now use the grid to plan gamelike situations after they analyze the requirements of any game. Upon reaching a particular mastery criterion level (which you determine), the players are ready for the next step.

Step three is the playing of the desired game. Following the example used already in this chapter, a games teacher would engage the players in a basketball game. The game can be the traditional game or you can ask the players to engage in a modified version. This last statement is not inconsistent with comments

*Bette Logsdon et al. *Physical Education For Children: A Focus on the Teaching Process* (Philadelphia: Lea and Febiger, 1977).

TABLE 4-1.
PLAYER WEAVE

Players	Equipment	Movements	Organ. Pattern	Limitations	Purpose
3 players per group	1 ball and 3 hula hoops per group	dribbling a ball, weaving in and out of hoops, chest and bounce passes	weaving pattern around 3 hula hoops placed in a file pattern	1. All players need to continually run in and around hoops maintaining equal distance from one another. 2. Players dribble a ball when they receive a pass from a teammate. 3. Continue until a group scores 10 passes without dropping one!	Enhance motor skills. Maintain player position. Learn how to make movement adjustments with the body in a game-like situation.

made during the gamelike section. Rather, step three is really the combination of steps one and two into a formally structured game.

Step four now suggests that the players engage totally in the entire games analysis process that has been described in previous chapters.

This rather simple process (step one to four) really improves the efficiency of game players. How long players should spend on each step is dependent upon the desired outcome as well as the time it takes them to reach mastery competency that *you* establish for each of the steps. Barrett and Logsdon present some additional ideas and possible lesson plans in their book. (See footnote on page 72.) This author presents lessons, tasks, and planning procedures in another book.* Using these ideas, as well as ideas of your own, will lead to efficient games play.

---

*G. S. Don Morris. *Elementary Physical Education—Toward Inclusion.* (Salt Lake City: Brighton Publishing Company, 1980).

Chapter

Observation
and Assessment
Alternatives

Consistent with the philosophy of games analysis, it is important to be able to observe youngsters at play while looking for specific types of physical behavior. If it is important to consider the individual abilities of youngsters in a game environment, then one needs to observe and assess the movement of each individual. This suggests that the youngsters only need to know how they are doing individually, i.e., relative to themselves rather than in comparison to group norms.

Two new concepts relative to observation and evaluation procedures employed in an elementary physical education setting are therefore presented. Learning to control individual body parts, body segments, and then the entire body is a prerequisite to efficient movement behavior. Concern yourself with how much body and movement control each child exhibits while jumping and running rather than with how far one youngster jumped or how fast another can run 40 yards. If youngsters can initially demonstrate control of their movements, then movement for maximum performance (how fast, how far) will be greatly enhanced over time. Because youngsters display a maximum performance in a given movement behavior, this does not necessarily provide information relative to the mechanical efficiency of their movement patterns. They may be performing a skill in a significantly incorrect, i.e., mechanically inefficient, manner which affects performance. By changing the mechanical inefficiency you might be able to improve the child's total movement capability.

For years in physical education we have administered tests which measure performance. Examples of items on these tests are: number of sit-ups performed in 30 seconds, number of pull-ups, number of laps run in 12 minutes. The reason we do this is quite simple—it is easy to measure and record this type of information. This information does not necessarily allow the teacher to understand how or why a youngster moves in a particular manner. If we profess to care about individual development and if we profess to teach the individual, then we need a method of observing and evaluating individual performance in terms of motor control quality rather than maximum performance quality. To do this the teacher must be provided with techniques for observing a youngster for motor control. This requires a radical shift in thinking and observation technique.

The first step is to look at the individual performers as separate entities rather than observe the product of their movement. For example, observe a youngster's total bodily movements while throwing a ball rather than observing where the ball was thrown. Look at the youngster's total bodily movements while performing a lay-up in basketball rather than observing whether or not the ball went in the hoop. In order to help youngsters improve their skill performance you must be able to provide them with adequate sound directions that will allow the youngsters to make adjustment in their movement behavior in order that the ball go through the hoop. Does the coach who yells "Try harder, hang in there!" provide the performer with adequate information that will produce a better performance next time? This strategy of observing the performer rather than the performance outcome is difficult to learn, and it does take time. However, with constant reminders to yourself, the strategy can be developed. Once this has occurred it is time to move to the next step.

The second step is to begin to observe the individual body parts rather than the total movement of the body. Observe general body segments and then the individual body part. For example, when a youngster is beginning to learn how to throw a ball efficiently look at the lower body segment (waist to feet). Specifically identify which foot the youngster is stepping forward with. Arm-leg opposition should be exhibited—step forward with left leg if throwing right-handed.

It is far more important to observe what a youngster is currently doing in a movement task than to concentrate attention and advice on what is *not* being done. The reason for this is that the teacher first needs to understand what the performer is able to do in order to be able to identify where the youngster is on the developmental sequence within the skill and finally prescribe the next movement task. This presupposes that each teacher knows the developmental sequences of the basic motor patterns, e.g., throwing, catching, kicking, jumping, running, striking. It is not the purpose of this book to provide that information, but it is suggested that all interested teachers examine Ralph Wickstrom's *Fundamental Motor Patterns* (1977) for further information.

Now that we possess the strategies to observe youngsters' ability to control their movement patterns, let us apply the concept to the motor patterns of throwing and the standing long jump.

THROWING

First, look at the entire movement pattern, and then look at the legs in relation to the youngster's throwing arm. Many first and second graders will step forward with the foot on the same side as the throwing arm, i.e., right foot forward, right-handed thrower. This is an immature pattern of throwing, so simply tell the youngster to step forward with the left foot next time. Also watch how close to or far away from the head the ball is held when the arm is cocked, i.e., brought back prior to throwing the ball. The ball should be close to the head in order to control it. Look at the youngster's hips and shoulders. Both body parts should rotate away from the target or to the right side with the shoulders rotating 1½ times the distance the hips rotate. Have any youngster who is not doing this practice rotating the hips and shoulders, first without the ball and then with the ball.

STANDING LONG JUMP

First, look at the youngster's entire bodily movement pattern. Next, look at the feet. It is common to see youngsters move their feet to a stagger position just before jumping—this is inefficient. Tell them to keep both feet still before jumping. Next, the youngsters' arms as they prepare to jump and also during the jump. Many youngsters will not swing their arms like a pendulum to provide arm force—they simply let their arms dangle at their sides. They can play an arm swinging game just to get them swinging the arms—don't let them jump. After a few trials in which they demonstrate their swinging ability let them perform the whole task of jumping.

The above remarks did not cover all of the body parts that you as a teacher should watch, but the few instances given should enable you to begin observing youngsters' performance critically and from the point of view of motor control. One last comment should perhaps be made relative to motor control, and that is that the structure of the task we ask youngsters to do dramatically dictates whether they will exhibit the kind of movement pattern desired. Take the following example:

> If you want a youngster to exhibit a mature throwing pattern, ask him to throw a ball against a wall rather than to play catch with a partner standing six feet away. In asking the youngster to perform the latter task, you are really telling him to get the ball to his partner so that he doesn't drop it. Thus he will throw in the best way he knows to get the ball to his partner.
>
> This concept has implications for use of equipment. It would be too rough on school walls to have the children throw hard type balls, so simply use nylon balls, i.e., balls made from nylons, to throw against the wall. In addition, these nylon balls won't bounce a half-mile away from the children, so they can spend most of their time practicing throwing rather than practicing retrieving.
>
> If you don't want the standing long jumper to exhibit an inefficient jumping pattern, eliminate how far he jumps until he can perform the task under control.
>
> Finally, if you want a youngster to practice just the action of kicking, use half-gallon milk cartons. Ask the children to kick the milk carton rather than a ball. Have you ever kept track of the time a youngster spends in retrieving a ball that he has kicked versus the amount of time spent on kicking? This again is a classic example of how the structure of a task affects motor outcome, specifically retrieval versus movement time. Movement time is nothing more than the time you allow a youngster to move or practice a task.

ASSESSMENT TOOL

Observation strategies have been presented, but it is now important to discuss how you will discover whether you are doing what you think you are doing with the youngsters. This falls within the area of assessment.

Assessment should be used for diagnosis and prescription of movement behavior, and for nothing else. An assessment tool should provide you with information which identifies why a youngster is behaving in a certain way, and from this you should be able to provide the students with helpful information so that they can improve their motor performance.

Games can provide movement experiences that aid in the development of motor skills. In order to develop the motor skills within a game framework, one must structure the game appropriately, which means that one must be able to identify the factors that influence the development of that skill and present the movement tasks in parts that each learner can reasonably cope with. Thus a use of the games analysis grid is to design a series of games adopting a task and factor analysis format. We will examine the factor analysis concept as it is applied to game design.

Let us examine the motor behavior of striking in terms of the factors that seem to influence its level of performance by elementary students. The chart on the next page (Table 5-1) identifies several, but not all, of these factors.

The chart shows some of the factors identified as affecting the motor performance of striking. Within each factor a degree of difficulty continuum has been established from easy to more difficult as the directional arrows indicate. For example, after analyzing the striking implement factor, research and experience have shown that it is easiest to strike an object with one's hand. It is a bit more difficult to strike an object with a paddle and most difficult to strike it with a bat. Research by Bruce (1966) and Williams (1968) suggests that youngsters can first visually track a horizontally moving object, then they can track a vertically moving object, and finally, around age nine or ten, most youngsters can efficiently track an object travelling through a variety of planes or in an arc. It is suggested that a larger object is easier to strike than a small object when first learning this motor behavior. Available research also indicates that it is easier to strike an object that travels to your preferred side than one that travels to your nonpreferred side. An object travelling directly at the performer is the most difficult to strike. Moran (1975) recently completed a study indicating that the ball color influenced the ability of elementary youngsters to exhibit efficient striking behavior. He found that the youngsters were able to strike the blue balls best, then yellow, and finally white balls. When designing a movement task you definitely should consider the visibility of the object, and the ball

TABLE 5-1.
FACTORS INFLUENCING MOTOR BEHAVIOR OF STRIKING

Striking Implement	Trajectory of Object Being Struck	Size of Object Being Struck	Object Direction in Flight	Weight of Object Being Struck	Color of Object Being Struck	Anticipation Location	Speed Object Is Travelling
Hand	Horizontal	Large	Right	Light	Blue	How far must the performer move before striking the object	Slow
↓	↓	↓	↓	↓	↓		↓
Paddle	Vertical	Small	Left	Heavy	Yellow		Fast
↓	↓		↓		↓		
Bat	Arc		Center		White		

color and background seem to influence the efficiency of the striking action. The closer the object is to the performer, the easier it is for him to strike it, and efficiency of striking decreases the farther the object is away from the performer. Most of the preceding information is nothing more than common sense which recently has been supported by research. A teacher can now design movement tasks and games that allow each task and game to account for current stages of motor development by the students. The ability to account or identify what stage each student is at suggests that there exists a procedure for assessing these stages. A simple assessment tool called a movement profile sheet indicates what each student's ability is within a single factor or any combination of striking factors. Below is a sample motor profile sheet (Table 5-2) that has analyzed and demonstrated the striking ability a student has exhibited while considering the interaction of two factors— striking implement and size of the object being struck.

TABLE 5-2.
MOTOR PROFILE OF STRIKING ABILITY

	S_1	S_2	S_3	S_4
I_1	Succeeded on 1-8	Succeeded on 1-9	Succeeded on 1-17	Succeeded on 1-23
I_2	Tried but failed 1-8	Succeeded on 1-10	Succeeded on 1-22	Failed on 1-23
I_3	Tried but failed 1-8	Tried but failed 1-10	Tried but failed 1-22	Failed on 1-23
I_4				Failed on 1-23

S = size of object		I = striking implement	
S_1 = 12" balloon		I_1 = hand	
S_2 = 10" plastic beach ball		I_2 = paddle	
S_3 = 8" rubber ball		I_3 = racquet	
S_4 = 4" rubber ball		I_4 = whiffle bat	

The profile sheet on the opposite page (Table 5-3) is easier to read if you only put the date in the appropriate space upon successful completion of the task, as demonstrated.

TABLE 5-3.
PROFILE SHEET

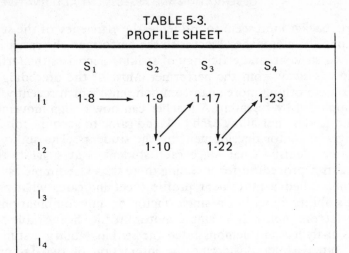

The teacher establishes the criteria for successful completion of the task. For example, in Box S_1, I_1, the criteria might be: "Hit a 12" balloon with your hand in a forward direction three times in succession." It is up to you to decide upon the criteria to assess successful completion of the task. Try not to influence the task by adding the influence of yet another factor. This profile sheet also indicates to the teacher which of the two factors under investigation influenced this particular student's striking ability. Which factor was it—size of the object or striking implement? By observation, the striking implement seems to be the more limiting factor of the two simply because the student was able to strike all the sizes of the object but could only strike with a hand or a paddle. This information is important for the teacher because now the teacher knows why a student demonstrates a particular kind of motor performance. Thus in a game form this particular student should be allowed to use a hand or a paddle to strike with. More than likely if he uses a bat he will not be successful.

Another service the profile sheet provides is that it gives the teacher specific directions in which to go in designing motor tasks. Knowing the student's current motor status and the factor or factors influencing successful performance, the teacher should now be able to help him improve his motor performance. Having been given appropriate tasks, the student should improve in his ability to perform. When assessing a motor skill, the teacher needs to account for all the factor interactions rather than just settling for a two-factor interaction, i.e., it would be appropriate to investigate the student's striking ability when one, two, or three other factors are considered. The profile sheet opposite (Table 5-4) illustrates the point.

With such a profile sheet, the teacher can look at a youngster's striking ability as three factors influence performance. Moreover, the teacher is now beginning to get more and more information regarding the youngster's ability to exhibit striking behavior. The teacher can analyze any motor behavior using this concept and can choose to identify as many of the factors that influence the specific motor behavior as seem necessary. This new assessment technique presupposes that: (a) one is able to identify the factors that influence a motor behavior; (b) one is able to design movement tasks within each factor on an easy to more difficult continuum; (c) one has a variety of equipment; and (d) one knows the classroom mechanics of administering the concept.

To illustrate the above, the following is a personal identification of the factors that seem to affect the motor behaviors of striking, catching, kicking, and throwing:

1. Size of object
2. Color of object
3. Trajectory of object
4. Weight of object
5. Speed of object
6. Color of background
7. Anticipation location
8. Texture of object
9. Illumination level
10. Illumination type
11. Object direction in flight relative to performer
12. Speed of performance by student.

There are undoubtedly many more factors that can be identified, but they must be left for another book. Most of the above-mentioned factors do not affect throwing, although Nos.1 and 3 (being thrown), 4 and 5 (speed of object being thrown), 8 and 12 seem to influence the throwing behavior. The color of a ball and background affecting the skill of catching is supported by Morris (1974) in recent research where blue, yellow, and white balls against a black, white background produced the best catching results in the order listed. Both Morris and Moran (1975) have

TABLE 5-4.
PROFILE SHEET

	W₁			W₂			W₃			W₄		
	C_1	C_2	C_3	C_1	C_2	C_3	C_1	C_2	C_3	C_1	C_2	C_3
V_1	8-2			8-6			8-8			9-1	9-3	9-4
V_2		8-4		8-7					8-10			
V_3												
V_4												

C_1 = blue ball
C_2 = yellow ball
C_3 = white ball

V_1 = slow travelling-20 ft/sec
V_2 = 25 ft/sec
V_3 = 30 ft/sec
V_4 = 35 ft/sec

W_1 = lightest ball - 3 oz.
W_2 = light ball - 5 oz.
W_3 = heavy ball - 6 oz.
W_4 = heaviest ball - 8 oz.

suggested that more research be done in this area of object visibility. In the near future, therefore, it should be possible to provide teachers with additional information that should aid them in providing the optimal learning climate for motor skill development. Using simple logic, it is fairly easy to design movement tasks within each factor on a continuum basis. The profile sheet will tell you if the task design is out of proper sequence. For example, if the 30 students in your class were asked to hit a ball with the implements shown in Table 5-5 and the profile shown there resulted, you, the teacher, would know that the task had not been properly sequenced.

TABLE 5-5.
PROFILE SHEET

		I_1	I_2	I_3	I_4
Student	1	X	X	X	X
	2	X	X	X	X
	3	X	X	X	X
	4	X	X		X
	5	X	X		X
	6	X	X		X
	7	X	X		X
	8	X	X		

I_1 = hand
I_2 = paddle
I_3 = racquet
I_4 = fat bat

Because most of the students could strike the ball with implements 1, 2, and 4 but only a few could do so with implement 3, the teacher should switch implements 3 and 4 on the continuum so that the students use the fat bat before using the racquet.

It is not necessary for each teacher to have a lot of equipment in order to institute this concept, but sequencing the tasks with the available equipment, in the proper order, should result in more efficient teaching and learning. Over the years teachers should add to their supply of equipment in order to provide a choice for the students. You can buy inexpensive plastic balls in supermarkets, save the bladders of old, worn-out basketballs, keep the broken bats, racquets, and broom handles. All of these items can provide you with graduated equipment that allows each student to start with tasks that are easy and proceed developmentally to more difficult tasks.

Administration of the motor profile is quite simple. Each teacher can administer the assessment concept either in groups or individually. Provide a station or stations that assess specific performance in your own gym. The youngsters can administer the task for the specific motor behavior either individually or in a group. With third and fourth graders, fifth and sixth graders can be used as the assessors at these assessment stations. Parents, other teachers, or the youngsters themselves can self-administer the tasks in the upper grades. They must be taught the task administration procedures and the teacher must develop an environment of mutual trust in the gym if self-administration is to work. Experience has shown that youngsters will not be dishonest if they are given the opportunity to demonstrate honest behavior. The learning environment that requires individual analysis rather than individual comparison to group standing will promote a positive response to self-administration of the profile sheet. Because the motor profile concept is, by design, concerned with each individual's performance rather than with a comparative-position performance (individual's placement relative to group), it lends itself to the exhibition of honest behavior by students.

It is, however, important not to misuse this concept. We would be defeating the profile's purpose if we were to attempt to attach a letter grade to a youngster's performance within the profile sheet. The profile is intended to state each individual's current movement status, assessing the factors that most affect each individual's performance and offering direction for the teaching of the motor behavior. The profile concept is for the individual and concerns itself with the individual's progress. The following example illustrates how a teacher or administrator can misuse the motor profile assessment concept.

A teacher is teaching the skill of throwing to his class. The assessment tool is similar to the tool mentioned previously in the text. He is presently assessing the influence of two factors upon the skill of throwing. He makes the following remark: "If you can perform the task at L_3, B_4 you will get an A+. Likewise successful performance of L_1, B_3 gets you an A−;

depending upon what box you end up in, this determines your grade."

	L_1	L_2	L_3	L_4
B_1		C		C^+
B_2	B–	B		B^+
B_3	A–		A	
B_4			A^+	

This example represents *MISUSE* of the concept. It is not important to get a letter grade because the grade does not account for growth data, factor analysis data, etc. The teacher wants to know where the student is as an individual. Please, therefore, don't misuse the concept.

Another way to misuse this concept is to stop evaluating the factors that affect motor performance. One needs to continue to keep abreast of current research that suggests the relationship certain factors have with competent performance of basic movement behaviors. Teachers should also evaluate their factor analysis progressions within tasks in order to make sure that the tasks presented are actually aiding the performer.

Games analysis can incorporate the task analysis concept quite easily. A teacher can design a series of games that provides for progressive improvement in selected motor behaviors by focusing upon one, two, three or more factors that influence said motor behaviors.

EXAMPLE: You want to enhance the development of catching and kicking skills in your class. Each youngster works individually to develop motor competency in catching and kicking and they now are ready to use these skills in a game form. As the teacher you have identified certain factors that affect the performance of these two skills. (See Table 5-6.)

Movement profiles have been established for both motor skills which look at only two factors at a time. (See p. 89.)

TABLE 5-6.
KICKING FACTORS

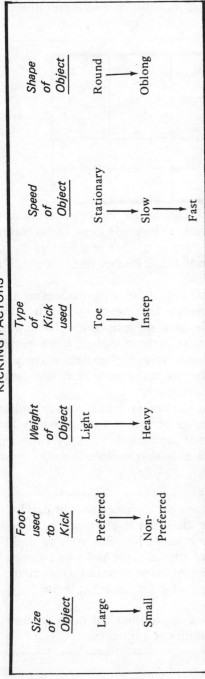

Size of Object	Foot used to Kick	Weight of Object	Type of Kick used	Speed of Object	Shape of Object
Large → Small	Preferred → Non-Preferred	Light → Heavy	Toe → Instep	Stationary → Slow → Fast	Round → Oblong

CATCHING FACTORS

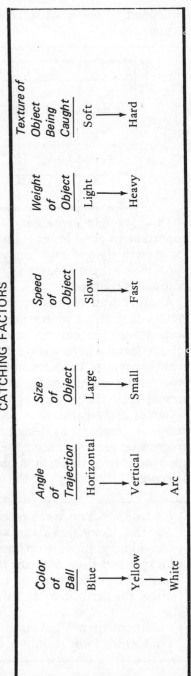

Color of Ball	Angle of Trajection	Size of Object	Speed of Object	Weight of Object	Texture of Object Being Caught
Blue → Yellow → White	Horizontal → Vertical → Arc	Large → Small	Slow → Fast	Light → Heavy	Soft → Hard

KICKING PROFILE SHEET

Size of Object (S)   Weight of Object (W)

Easy- Difficult

	S_1	S_2	S_3	S_4
Easy				
W_1				
W_2				
W_3				
W_4				

Difficult

W_1 = 6 oz. ball		S_1 = largest ball - 18" diameter
W_2 = 8 oz. ball		S_2 = large ball - 14" diameter
W_3 = 12 oz. ball		S_3 = small ball - 12" diameter
W_4 = 16 oz. ball		S_4 = smallest ball - 8" diameter

CATCHING PROFILE SHEET

Texture of Object (T)   Angle of Trajection (A)

Easy ⟶ Difficult

	T_1	T_2	T_3	T_4
A_1				
A_2				
A_3				

T_1 = fleece ball		A_1 = horizontal plane
T_2 = nerf ball		A_2 = vertical plane
T_3 = nylon ball		A_3 = ball travels in arc
T_4 = whiffle ball		

162694

TABLE 5-7.
GAMES GRID

Game	Players	Organ. Pattern	Equipment	Movement	Limitations	Purpose
1	3/team	Random	*Kicking-S_1 W_1 Catching-T_1	Kicking-Toe Kick Catching-A_1	Teacher designed	Develop catching and kicking skills
2			Kicking-S_2 W_2 Catching-T_2	Kicking-Same Catching-A_2		
3			Kicking-S_2 W_3 Catching-T_3	Kicking-Same Catching-A_3		
4			Kicking-S_3 W_3 Catching-T_4	Kicking-Same Catching-A_3		
5			Kicking-S_3 W_4 Catching-T_4	Kicking-Same Catching-A_3		

*Refer to profile sheets on p. 89.

Table 5-7 illustrates how to apply the motor profile information to the games analysis grid.

Having done all of the preceding, you either design games or adapt current games so that you progressively allow the preceding factors to dominate the game design.

You have now, with each new game, built upon the previous game's factors. Table 5-7 is only an example. You, of course, will adjust the game design to meet the individual's needs. In addition, you could design into each game several other factors that influence the skills being worked on. Simply by referring to the youngsters' profile sheets you can design games appropriate to their movement needs and capabilities.

Let's look at a typical fifth grader's profile sheet and then design a game utilizing the information on the sheet. For the sake of the discussion, our fifth grader will be named Lisa. Again, let's look at the skills of catching and kicking and specifically analyze only two factors that affect each of the motor skills.

CATCHING PROFILE SHEET

Texture of Object (T)   Angle of Trajection (A)

Easy ───────────────────→ Difficult

NAME___Lisa_____

	T_1	T_2	T_3	T_4
A_1	10-2			
A_2		10-10		
A_3			11-2	11-8

T_1 = fleece ball A_1 = horizontal plane
T_2 = nerf   ball A_2 = vertical plane
T_3 = nylon   ball A_3 = ball travels in arc
T_4 = whiffle ball

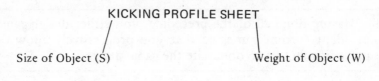

KICKING PROFILE SHEET

Size of Object (S)   Weight of Object (W)

Easy ───────────────►Difficult

NAME___Lisa_____

	S₁	S₂	S₃	S₄
W₁	10-2			
W₂		10-10		
W₃			11-2	11-8
W₄				

W₁ = 6 oz. ball	S₁ = largest ball - 18" diameter
W₂ = 8 oz. ball	S₂ = large ball - 14" diameter
W₃ = 12 oz. ball	S₃ = small ball - 12" diameter
W₄ = 16 oz. ball	S₄ = smallest ball - 8" diameter

The dates in each profile sheet represent the dates Lisa successfully completed the appropriate movement task. Both Lisa and the teacher know what Lisa is capable of doing when she is asked to kick or catch a ball. The teacher can now design a game that will enhance development of these skills to meet Lisa's needs. Using the games analysis grid, here's what a game might look like using the information garnered from the motor profile sheets. (See Table 5-8.)
Description:
Batting Team—The batting team is up for only two minutes, then they go to the field. The batting team divides into two groups of four players with one group at bat at a time—the

TABLE 5-8.
KICK AND GO

Name of Game	Players	Organ. Pattern	Equipment	Movement	Limitations	Purpose
Kick and Go	8 per team	Random in field; hula hoops in circle	kicking ball of choice; catching ball of choice	kicking catching running throwing	1. Kick ball of choice into field. 2. Run as group of 4 around all 7 bases before fielding team completes task. 3. Fielding team must have one person retrieve kicked ball, place it in hula hoop at center of field. 4. Once this is done, all other fielding players stand inside hoop, pick up ball and play self catch for 7 catches—ball must go above shoulders. 5. Complete this task before runners cross the home plate for out. 6. Time limit game—batting team up for 2 minutes only.	To develop kicking and catching skills.

groups alternate batting. One player in the group kicks the ball rolled by the teacher; this player, along with the other three group members, runs around all the seven bases and returns to home base. If the last member of the batting group crosses home plate before the fielding team completes its task, they score one run. Then the next group bats.

Fielding Team—Players start outside their hula hoops. Once the ball is kicked, the player closest to the kicked ball retrieves it and returns it to a hula hoop found in the center of the field. Once this is accomplished, all the fielding players stand inside their own hula hoops, pick up their balls, and play vertical catch seven times with themselves. The ball must go above their shoulders. If they can do all of this before the last person in the batting group crosses home plate, then an out is registered. After 2 minutes' time, the two teams switch places.

Lisa would have her choice of balls to kick, choosing one that she is capable of kicking, and she would have her own ball to play catch with when she is out in the field. Each of these balls would change from 10-2 to 11-8 within this particular game. This then is an example of how games analysis can make use of information provided by movement profile sheets.

This idea may suggest to some that a lot of time be spent in preparing lessons and also that it is necessary to have a lot of equipment. Again, use the equipment you now have, attempt to get more, and start designing movement profile sheets and alternative games. It takes only a few hours to design profile sheets, put them on a stencil, and run off several dozen. Only attempt to use this concept initially with maybe one sport or just a couple of motor skills. Slowly over the weeks and months expand the concept to other movement areas or games. If you believe that the motor development of your students is important you will spend the extra minutes to become a precision movement teacher. Remember, there is nothing sacred about the game design Lisa played. As a matter of fact, there are many more versions of the game the youngsters could be asked to play. Likewise, there is nothing sacred about the number of choices allowed for each identified factor affecting a motor behavior. Although S_1-S_4 and W_1-W_4 choices were shown in the kicking profile sheet, there are obviously more choices available—it all depends on the type and amount of equipment you have.

Finally, in the appendix at the back of this book there are a number of examples of choices allowed for several factors that affect performance of selected motor behaviors. Remember that they are examples and should by no means be regarded as complete.

References

Bruce, Russell. "The Effects of Variations in Ball Trajectory upon the Catching Performance of Elementary School Children." Ph.D. dissertation, University of Wisconsin, 1966.

Keogh, Jack. Section entitled "Development in Fundamental Motor Tasks" in *A Textbook of Motor Development* by Charles B. Corbin. Dubuque, Iowa: Wm. C. Brown, 1973.

Moran, Gary. "The Effect of Ball Color and Background Color on the Striking Performance of Second, Fourth, and Sixth Grade Children." Ph.D. dissertation, University of Oregon, 1975.

Morris, Gordon S. "The Effects Ball Color and Background Color Have upon the Catching Performance of Second, Fourth, and Sixth Grade Youngsters." Ph.D. dissertation, University of Oregon, 1974.

Morris, Gordon S. "Equipment Color: A Limiting Factor." *JOHPER* 46 (June 1975):8.

Wickstrom, Ralph. *Fundamental Motor Patterns.* Philadelphia: Lea and Febiger, 1970.

Williams, Harriet. "The Effects of Systemic Variation of Speed and Direction of Object Flight and of Skill and Age Classification upon Visuoperceptual Judgement of Moving Object in Three-dimensional Space." Ph.D. dissertation, University of Wisconsin, 1968.

Chapter

Examples of Games Designed for Specific Movement Areas

This chapter will provide the reader with examples of games from which it is hoped more games will be designed to meet the needs of developing children. All of the games presented have been either played or designed by the youngsters themselves. The format of this chapter will be as follows:

1. Section on softball, volleyball, basketball, and active academic games.
2. Within these sections, where appropriate, games for elementary school students and secondary students will be presented.

The order of game presentation does not reflect any progression in terms of development—the games are simply representative of the hundreds of games developed during the past seven years by either the writer or his students.

SOFTBALL TYPE GAMES

In designing a game of this type you must remember that the visual-perception system may influence the kinds of movements a youngster is capable of performing. You will notice in most of the softball games that movements other than those which are an integral part of the game are included within the game structure.

Remember, you can substitute or alter any component within the structure of these games. By simply changing the major movement task from hitting to kicking you have developed seven

(go to page 111)

GAME 6-1. WORKUP (ELEMENTARY)

Players	Equipment	Movements	Organ. Pattern	Limitations	Purpose
1 - 8 Can be played with as few as 3 players	bat, balls of various types	hitting, running, fielding, catching, bowling	somewhat random—1 batter—1 pitcher—rest are fielders	1. Batter stays at bat until a fielding player hits the bat on ground or until a fielder catches a fly ball. 2. Batting rotation follows: current batter, upon an out, moves to outfield, pitcher moves to batter, a fielder moves to pitcher. 3. If batter can catch the ball after it hits the bat but before the ball hits the ground he remains at bat. 4. Upon successful catch of a fly ball, the catcher changes places with the batter and the batter assumes the fielder's position in the rotation	To develop fielding and tracking skills.

Description: A batter hits the ball toward the fielders. He then places the bat on the ground. The fielder rolls the ball toward the bat; if he hits it, then everyone moves up one position. If he doesn't, the batter continues hitting the ball.

ONE BASE

GAME 6-2. ONE BASE (ELEMENTARY)

Players	Equipment	Movements	Organ. Pattern	Limitations	Purpose
2 teams 5-10 per team	bat, balls, one base	hitting, fielding, running, throwing, and catching	X - players 0 - base - home plate - - - thrown bat boundaries	1. Two outs/inning or 5 run limit, then teams switch positions. 2. Teacher is pitcher. 3. Stay at bat until batter hits ball—fair ball anywhere ball is hit. 4. To get an out you must: (a) catch a fly or catch a ball after one bounce (b) tag runner out with ball (c) get ball to base before runner gets to base. 5. Thrown bat by hitter outside boundaries is an out. 6. Runner may stay at base, return upon next hit. 7. Base is 30' - 40' from home plate.	To develop basic softball skills plus introduce base running strategies.

Description: This game is similar to regular softball except it has only one base quite a distance from home plate. The batting team, one member at a time, goes to bat until batter hits the ball. Batter runs to the base, either stays or returns—depends on the situation. To score a run the batter must return to home plate and touch it. The fielders play in the field as in regulation softball. When 2 outs or 5 runs are scored, the teams trade jobs. Play as long as you like.

GAME 6-3. MAGLADRY BALL (ELEMENTARY)

Players	Equipment	Movements	Organ. Pattern	Purpose
4-12 per team	1 batting tee, 4 bowling pins, hula hoop for each fielder, 3 different types of balls	running, hitting, bowling, catching, throwing	bowling pins X X X X X X X X center hoop- batting tee - out plate X-represents fielder -home plate O-represents hula hoop	To develop running, hitting, bowling, catching, throwing skills. To promote team strategy.

Limitations:

1. Time limit game—batting team up for 1½ mins. only.
2. How to make an out: the only way to make an out is to perform specific tasks as fielders, get on special ball to out plate before batter crosses home.
3. Batter's job: hit plastic ball off of batting tee, run to bowling pin area. Stay behind line (10' from pins) and bowl a ball until all pins are knocked over. Then run to home plate.
4. Fielders: after batter hits the ball, one player retrieves the ball, rest of players stand inside hoop—throw the retrieved ball to 7 different players—if the ball is dropped, start the count all over again—person receiving the 7th throw runs to the center hoop and places the ball inside the out hoop—it must stay in the hoop—if all of this is done before batter crosses home, the batter is out!

GAME 6-4. MAGLADRY BALL PLUS (ELEMENTARY)

Players	Equipment	Movements	Organ. Pattern	Purpose
same as game 6-3	same as game 6-3 except no bowling equipment, need several more hula hoops	same as game 6-3		same as game 6-3

Limitations:

1. Same as game 6-3.
2. Same as game 6-3.
3. Batter's job: hit plastic ball off batting tee, batter runs to "go thru hoop" (15'-20' from batting tee), holds hoop perpendicular to floor—rest of teammates must run through the hoop; all these players must then run and cross home plate.
4. Fielder's job: same as game 6-3 except the player receiving the 7th throw simply runs the ball to the out hoop.
5. If the fielding team gets the ball to the out hoop before everyone on the batting team has crossed home plate, an out is registered.

Description: The limit category describes this game and game 6-3 quite adequately. By designing the game in this manner you increase the movement time and decrease the waiting time quite considerably for each player. Simply by changing the game this much you begin to eliminate inappropriate social behavior that is exhibited by players who have to stand around and wait their turn. Although this concept is introduced now, feel free to apply it to other types of games with a similar design. By mandating that it is a time limit game, you eliminate one team staying at bat for the whole play time. This concept also influences the kinds of social sanctions that result when a team stays in the field the whole time and can't ever seem to get up to bat.

MAGLADRY BALL

GAME 6-5. HIT AND GO (ELEMENTARY)

Players	Equipment	Movements	Organ. Pattern	Limitations		Purpose
same as game 6-3 but each batting team divides into 2 groups	same as game 6-3 except hula hoops represent bases	same as game 6-3	Random in field before ball is hit—after ball is hit, fielding team lines up in a file X X X X	1. Same as game 6-3 2. Same as game 6-3 3. Batter's job—hit the ball and run around 6 bases set in field like regular softball game—return home before the ball gets to out hoop. Batting team is divided into 2 groups—groups alternately bat—one member from each group bats and runs the bases, however the rest of the players in batter's batting group run the bases in a single file. 4. Fielder's job—one player fields the ball, rest of the fielders line up in a file with legs spread—the fielder with ball must crawl through teammates' legs carrying the ball—then runs the ball to the out hoop—if the ball reaches the out hoop before all of the batting group crosses home plate, an out is registered.	home plate	same as game 6-3

Description: This game is similar to games 6-3 and 6-4. The fielders begin in a random position in the field. After the ball is hit the fielding players line up one behind the other with their legs spread so the person retrieving the ball can finish the designed task. The batting team is divided equally into two groups, A and B. If A group is up (only one player hits), upon hitting the ball everyone in group A runs the bases in a single file. By splitting the batting team into two groups you now provide for some recovery time—this can become quite a strenuous game.

HIT AND GO

GAME 6-6. JUMP AND HIT (ELEMENTARY)

Players	Equipment	Movements	Organ. Pattern	Purpose
same as game 6-3	same as game 6-3 plus one jump rope	same as game 6-3 plus jumping rope		Same as game 6-3 plus enhance jumping rope behavior

Limitations:

1. Same as game 6-3.
2. Same as game 6-3.
3. Batter's job: Upon hitting the ball, run to jump rope which is placed at opposite end of gym or field—jump rope 10 times—run back to home plate.
4. Fielder's job: Same as game 6-3.

Description: This game is essentially the same as game 6-3 but it introduces another motor skill not commonly found in softball—jumping rope. It is important to understand that you may have to change the numbers. The youngsters could either pass the ball or jump rope. Use the numbers appropriate for your youngsters. There is nothing sacred about those given in the game description.

GAME 6-7. COMBINATION SOFTBALL (ELEMENTARY)

Players	Equipment	Movements	Organ. Pattern	Purpose
any manageable number per team	hula hoops crash pads basketballs balls	running hitting forward rolls basketball shooting		Promote development of the given motor skills plus begin to combine a variety of motor tasks

Limitations:

1. Similar to game 6-3 but increase batting time.
2. Same as game 6-3.
3. Batter must hit the ball and run to crash pads where he performs one, two, or three forward rolls—you choose—then he picks up basketball and stays until he scores 2 baskets, he then runs to home plate.
4. Same as game 6-3.

Description: The game is fairly self-descriptive. This game begins to combine a variety of movement tasks into a game. The game presupposes that each youngster has worked on the individual movement behaviors prior to their inclusion in a game form. This kind of game is excellent for getting the youngsters to think in alternatives relative to game design. This game also allows for individual interpretation of the tasks. For example, the task at the mats must be stated in the following manner: Perform any three forward type of rolls. Likewise the individual players are allowed to use any shooting style at the basketball area. Finally, this game has often been used to promote the design of many other games using skills not normally found in softball.

COMBINATION SOFTBALL

GAME 6-8. FIGURE 8 SOFTBALL (SECONDARY)

Players	Equipment	Movements	Organ. Pattern	Purpose
any manageable number per team	7 bases, 1 wooden stake, several types of bats, several types of balls	softball skills plus bowling in some cases	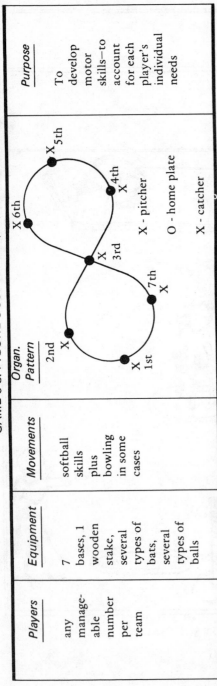 X - pitcher O - home plate X - catcher	To develop motor skills—to account for each player's individual needs

Limitations:

1. Four outs per ½ inning.
2. How to make an out: basically the same as traditional softball—catch a fly, get the ball to the base before the runner, tag runner out.
3. Batter can choose type of bat and type of ball used each time he comes to bat.
4. Throwing the bat is an automatic out.
5. Play 3 innings.
6. Stay at bat until you hit the ball forward.

Description: The game is played similarly to traditional softball. The batter runs all 7 bases in proper order—first base to 7th base in a figure 8 pattern as illustrated in the organizational pattern category. The major difference is that each batter chooses the ball and bat used plus dictates to the pitcher how the ball is delivered to the batter—rolled on the ground, thrown under-hand, etc. The batter then strikes the ball and runs to first base.

GAME 6-9. BADMINTON BASEBALL

Players	Equipment	Movements	Organizational Pattern	Limitations	Purpose
2 teams—unlimited numbers allowed on each team.	badminton racquet shuttlecock bases	running catching hitting throwing	Diamond Pattern X-2d 3rd-X X-1st O pitcher X-home	1. Each team only gets one out per inning. 2. Unlimited swings at shuttlecock—hit shuttlecock with racquet in fair territory. 3. Must run all the bases on each hit. 4. 1 run scores if you can run all bases. 5. Must tag runner out with shuttlecock. 6. Play 5 innings but each inning can last only 5 minutes per team.	Develop striking skills. Score most runs. Have fun without very many players on a team and without fancy equipment.

Badminton Baseball was designed by seven-year-old Karen Morris

GAME 6-9 (Continued)

Description: The game looks like regular baseball except badminton equipment is used. The batter can pitch to herself or have the shuttlecock pitched toward her. Upon hitting a fair "bird," batter runs all 3 bases and scores if she doesn't get tagged by defensive player who has the shuttlecock. Bases are very close together, close enough to make it around all bases with a good hit. My daughter also allows "ghosts" in the game (a batter can stay on one base, ghost takes her place). Other rules apply. Can you think what they may be?

new kickball games. Thus you have 14 "new" games that you can now play at the elementary level. Many of the games described have been played at the secondary level by teachers in Montana, and the feedback received from these teachers has been quite positive. Game 6-8 was designed by some of the writer's high school students.

This proved to be a most interesting game. The students actually designed a game that began to account for individual hitting abilities. "Johnny Athlete" chose to hit a regular ball, while "Clumsie Charlie" chose to have the ball rolled toward him. The next thing to happen was that the students realized it was all right to exhibit their current motor ability. They began to see that they were different in motor ability, but each player could be accepted within the game structure on his current merits of ability.

This game led to a number of other games. One game they designed was similar to game 6-8, but each runner could run to any base at any time in any order. The only rule was that they had to touch each base before returning home. Sometimes three people would be on a base at one time. Soon even those kids who disliked physical education were asking to extend the class time—the biggest problem became getting the students to their next class on time.

VOLLEYBALL TYPE GAMES

The general movement behaviors found in volleyball type games must first be identified if the skills required in these games are to be developed. Volleyball games require that a player strike a moving ball, therefore all of the games must include this striking behavior. It is preposterous to claim that one is promoting volleyball behavior by requiring a youngster to catch a ball and then throw it back over the net. This is not to say that this is not a good skill to learn; rather it is simply not a volleyball type of skill. One can include the catch-and-throw motor behavior in a game, but don't imagine that you will promote striking quickly. To develop the striking behavior you must require the students to strike at a ball. Yes, there are a multitude of factors that influence this skill; they must be accounted for in the game design. The following games are designed to promote volleyball skills, and it is hoped you can use them in your program.

The games described in this next section lead towards regulation volleyball. Many of the elementary games can be adapted to the secondary level as you will soon see.

GAME 6-10. KEEP IT GOING (ELEMENTARY)

Players	Equipment	Movements	Organ. Pattern	Limitations	Purpose
2 players per team	a ball of your choice	overhead striking underarm striking	pairs of players randomly scattered around gym	1. Must strike the ball in over head or underarm striking pattern. 2. You can hit it to yourself several times, then hit it to your partner. 3. You can play the ball off one bounce on the floor. 4. Try to keep the ball moving for 10 sec, 15 sec., 30 sec., teacher sets limit.	To enhance given motor skills. To promote coopera-tion among 2 players.

GAME 6-11. KEEP IT UP (ELEMENTARY)

Players	Equipment	Movements	Organ. Pattern	Limitations	Purpose
same as game 6-10				1. Same as game 6-10. 2. Same as game 6-10. 3. Must keep the ball off the floor. Once it hits the floor, couple retrieves the ball and sits down. 4. Must keep the ball up for a period of time or for a certain number of hits between the two players; e.g., 6 hits, 12 hits.	Same as game 6-10

Description: The game is self-explanatory. When first teaching the striking skill to these youngsters it is most important that they learn to control the ball. Therefore, the game is structured so the youngsters get the ball under control before they send it to their partner. The teacher controls the criteria determining when the game is over, i.e., certain number of hits or specific amount of time the ball must be kept off the floor.

GAME 6-12. KEEP IT UP OVER THE NET (ELEMENTARY)

Players	Equipment	Movements	Organ. Pattern	Limitations	Purpose
same as game 6-10	plus a net		couples facing each other with net between them	1. Same as game 6-10. 2. Same as game 6-10. 3. Same as game 6-11 plus you must strike it over the net to your partner so he can hit it back to you. 4. Same as game 6-11.	To develop net skills with a ball. To promote cooperative behavior.

Description: The addition of a net is the only difference between this game and the previous two games. Make sure that you vary the height of the net and slope of the net.

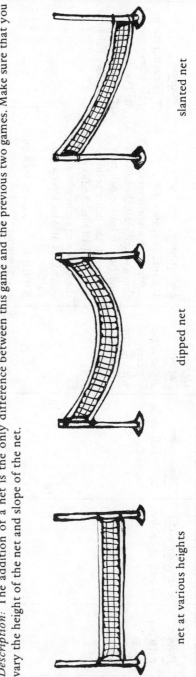

net at various heights   dipped net   slanted net

The height and slope variations allow the youngsters to pick the net type they can successfully cope with. There are dozens of versions of these three games—one can play each of the games with groups of 3, 4, 5, 6, players or more; likewise games 6-10 and 6-11 can be played with the players standing in a circle. You now have enough information to design several more games.

GAME 6-13. MASS VOLLEYBALL (ELEMENTARY)

Players	Equipment	Movements	Organ. Pattern	Limitations	Purpose
6-10 per team	ball of choice	volleyball, striking skills	2 teams facing each other with net between the two of them.	1. Same as game 6-10. 2. You can hit it several times to yourself then to a partner or hit the ball over the net to the other team. 3. If the ball hits the floor the opposing team gets a point regardless of who served the ball. 4. First team to score 10 points is the winner. 5. You cannot hit the net with your body—forfeit point if you do.	To develop team play using volleyball skills. To develop co-operative behavior.

Description: This game is played like regular volleyball except for the rule changes. There is no service area, so the person closest to the ball can serve it from their position. There are no prescribed positions, thus everyone is involved in the game.

GAME 6-14. THREE HITS (ELEMENTARY)

Players	Equipment	Movements	Organ. Pattern	Limitations	Purpose
same as game 6-13				1. Same as game 6-9. 2. A team can only hit the ball 3 times on one side and the ball must go over the net on the third hit—one player can hit it 3 times. 3. Same as game 6-12. 4. Same as game 6-12. 5. Same as game 6-12.	Same as game 6-13

Description: This game is similar to game 6-13 except now you are mandating that the players control the ball even more because the 3 hit limit suggests better control.

One can add an additional ball or two into games 6-13 and 6-14 if increased movement time per individual player is desired. Likewise, you can use a variety of ball types in these games. Elementary youngsters usually prefer the plastic balls or the inside of a basketball—the bladder. Do not hesitate to apply previously learned games analysis concepts when altering these games.

GAME 6-15. FOUR CORNERS VOLLEYBALL (ELEMENTARY)

Players	Equipment	Movements	Organ. Pattern	Purpose
3-6 players per team. 4 teams per net arrangement	4-6 balls per game	same as game 6-13	X X | X X X X | X X ——————— X X | X X X | X 2 nets crisscrossed with a team in each quadrant	To develop visual tracking behavior. To develop alertness in youngsters during game.

Limitations: All the rules are similar to games 6-13 and 6-14 except that initially no points are kept. Each team begins with one or two balls. The object is to play against the other three quadrants. See game description below.

Description: The players must be alert at all times. The object of the game is to have no balls in your quadrant. It is each team for themselves. Upon the go signal from the teacher, each team, using volleyball skills, attempts to get the balls to the other teams. The game looks almost like a free-for-all but the youngsters enjoy it very much. The teacher stops the game when one team seems to have the majority of the balls.

FOUR CORNERS VOLLEYBALL

GAME 6-16. FOUR HITS (SECONDARY)

Players	Equipment	Movements	Organ. Pattern	Limitations	Purpose
5-6 per team 2 teams per game	1 ball per game—you choose the ball	overhead and underarm striking skills	two teams facing each other with a net between the two of them.	1. Each player may hit the ball only once. 2. Each team may hit the ball only 4 times on one side and the ball must go over on the 4th hit. 3. If the ball hits the floor, the opposing team gets a point. 4. Ball must be served behind the service line (15'-20' from net). 5. Can only score when you are serving the ball. 6. If the non-serving team makes the ball hit the floor on the opposing team's side, the non-serving team "wins" the serve. 7. Game is 15 points.	To develop the given motor skills. To introduce volleyball rules. To promote cooperative team behavior.

Description: The game is played much like regulation volleyball. The major difference is that each team is allowed four hits on a side before sending the ball over to the other team. The purpose is quite simple. Allow the players to control the ball before hitting it.

GAME 6-17 is called THREE HITS—each team is allowed only 3 hits and then the ball must go over. Vary the type of ball used and height of the net when designing volleyball games for this age student.

GAME 6-18. SET AND SPIKE (SECONDARY)

Players	Equipment	Movements	Organ. Pattern	Limitations	Purpose
same as game 6-16		plus spike	↑	1. Same as game 6-16. 2. The ball may only be hit three times on one side; third hit needs to be a spike. 3. Same as game 6-16. 4. Same as game 6-16. 5. Same as game 6-16. 6. Same as game 6-16. 7. Same as game 6-16.	Same as game 6-16 plus teaching how to spike a ball.

Description: The only rule change is that the ball must be hit 3 times on a side with the third hit being a spike. The game looks like a traditional volleyball game.

GAME 6-19 simply introduces the circle rotation of the players upon receiving the serve. Otherwise the game is similar to traditional volleyball. Secondary students like to design other versions of this game using a variety of balls and other pieces of equipment.

BASKETBALL TYPE GAMES

This game area is perhaps the easiest one in which students can begin to modify the game structure. Experience at both the elementary and secondary level has shown that the students are capable of adapting equipment, altering rules, and even changing or adding additional movement patterns, and are willing or even eager to do so. All of the games described below have been played and enjoyed by the students. Some of them reflect the traditional form of basketball while others may not appear to you like a basketball game at all.

GAME 6-20. ONE X ONE (ELEMENTARY)

Players	Equipment	Movements	Organ. Pattern	Limitations	Purpose
2 per game	1 ball—you decide what kind. 1 hula hoop	all basketball movements	random, 1/2 court	1. NO traveling, double dribble. 2. Call own fouls, foul results in ball taken in from sidelines. 3. 3 pts. per basket. 4. 15 pts. wins game. 5. Winner of basket maintains possession. 6. 1 pt. per hula hoop score.	To develop shooting, dribbling, offensive and defensive skills.

Description: Game begins with one player inbounding ball. Offensive player may shoot at basket or at hula hoop hung from basket. Winner of basket maintains possession of ball. Play is similar to traditional basketball.

GAME 6-21. PASS AND SHOOT (ELEMENTARY)

Players	Equipment	Movements	Organ. Pattern	Limitations	Purpose
couples, unlimited	1 ball per couple	passing shooting	couples random in gym	1. Teacher indicates number of passes and shots to be taken per couple. 2. Must perform passes first, then one person performs prescribed number of shots, return to partner, sit down.	To develop pass and shooting skills.

Description: Couples face each other, 5' apart. Teacher writes large P & S on board with number under P & S. Players must then pass ball number indicated. One player shoots 'til basket is made. Return to partner, sit quietly.

This game promotes a great deal of movement time for passing and shooting. If you asked your students to practice passing the ball back and forth 50 times they would get very bored. However, putting the same movement task in a game form, I have found that the youngsters can perform 100-200 passes per session and still enjoy the game. The youngsters have altered the movement from the passing spot to the shooting area. For example, they suggested that you carry the ball, hop with the ball, run backwards with the ball, move in pairs passing the ball back and forth and many other movement tasks. They have also given the player who remains at the passing site a task to perform such as moving the ball in a figure 8 pattern around the legs. Can you share some ideas with us?

GAME 6-22. SHOOT AND GO

Number of Players	Equipment	Movements	Organizational Pattern	Limitations	Purpose
any number of players per team is allowed	1 basketball (any size) 1 backboard 1 hoop	running shooting jumping catching	X X X X X Foul line hoop	1. Must begin game by shooting from foul line—stay at foul line until you miss. 2. When you miss, rebound the ball, shoot from where you rebound the ball. 3. You get only 3 shooting attempts per shooting cycle, then it is another player's turn.	Put the ball into the basket. Enhance shooting skill. Score most points.

GAME 6-22 (Continued)

			4. Point system: 5 pts. if you make basket on first try; 3 pts. if you make a basket on 2nd try; 1 pt. if you make a basket on 3rd try; 1 pt. if rebound touches ground. 5. You end the game when you want to.	

Shoot and Go was designed by eleven-year-old Peter Morris.

Description: One person at a time engages in the 3-shot cycle. A player begins game taking a shot at the foul line. If player makes the shot, the player stays at the foul line for the second shot. If the player misses the basket, the ball must be rebounded before it touches the ground. The next shot is taken from where the ball is rebounded. Most points wins. Players take turns. Game over when everyone decides it's over.

GAME 6-23. FOUR CORNER RELAY (ELEMENTARY)

Players	Equipment	Movements	Organ. Pattern	Purpose
5-8/team	1 ball/team	dribbling passing		To develop dribbling skill.

Limitations:

1. Each team has first player dribble ball to gym center.
2. Must dribble ball with one hand.
3. May not bump into anybody or you must begin again.
4. First team to return to original starting position wins.
5. Must be sitting down.

Description: First person from each team dribbles to center of gym, all four crisscross one with the other. Each player continues diagonally to opposite corner of gym, hands ball off to next player who in turn dribbles to gym center. Original dribbler gets at end of line he has dribbled to. Play continues until all players return to starting position.

With this game you first have to ask your youngsters to run the pattern without the ball. The youngsters may be able to add a second ball for each team as they become more proficient.

Within the framework of this game, the youngsters have combined movement tasks or changed the movement directional order. Feel free to alter the game and come up with many more versions.

GAME 6-24. PASS AND TURN (ELEMENTARY)

Players	Equipment	Movements	Organ. Pattern	Purpose
4-8/team	1 ball/team	pass dribble	X X X X X X Columns facing other end of gym	To develop pass and dribble skills.

Limitations:

1. Each player may only dribble with one hand, must chest pass.
2. Each player must stop at designated spot on floor.
3. First team to have all players pass and turn wins.
4. Must be sitting on floor to end game.

Description: First player from each team dribbles ball to opposite end of gym, returns while dribbling ball to spot indicated on floor, performs chest pass to teammate who also dribbles to opposite end of gym, returns to mark on floor (5' from other player). He passes ball to first player who turns and passes to next person in line. This person and every other person in line must weave in and out of players standing on gym floor to other end of gym, return to spot on gym floor, pass to next player who passes to next and so on down the line until ball reaches starting column. Play continues until each player has dribbled ball and passed ball and is standing in line on gym floor.

PASS AND TURN

GAME 6-25. PASS, TURN AND SHOOT (ELEMENTARY)

Players	Equipment	Movements	Organ. Pattern	Purpose
same as game 6-24		plus shooting		Same as game 6-24 plus improving shooting skills.

Limitations:

1. Same as preceding game but add following rules: Each player, one at a time, gets to shoot at either basket (3 pts.) or at the hula hoop (1 pt.) hung from basket.
2. After shooting return via a dribble to next player in line.
3. Game is over when each player has shot once.
4. Most points win the game.
5. The shooting occurs after the pass and turn relay has been performed.

Description: Players perform pass and turn relay first. Then while standing in line one at a time the players try to score a basket via hula hoop or regular basket. Game is over when each person has taken one shot.

PASS, TURN AND SHOOT

GAME 6-26. BASKETBOWL (ELEMENTARY)

Players	Equipment	Movements	Organ. Pattern	Purpose
any number per team; do not have to have even numbers per team—the more teams you have, the greater is the movement time	variety of balls, hula hoops, bowling pins or something like them	all basketball movements plus bowling movements	relay formation--you decide--could be: X X X X X X X X X X X X X X X X X X X X X X X X X	To develop strategy. To promote motor skill development.

Limitations:

1. Time limit game—3 minutes.
2. Scoring system—1 point per pin knocked over, 2 points for putting ball through hula hoop, 3 points for putting ball through basket.
3. May only have one chance at bowling and may only take one shot at basket.
4. Must hand the ball to next player on your team.

Description: The teams are in any relay pattern you desire. The first player on each team attempts to bowl the ball and knock over a pin or pins set up 20'-30' away—preferably in front of wall. Having completed this task, the player retrieves the ball and moves (you decide) to the shooting area where he takes one shot at either the basket or the hula hoop hanging from the basket. He then gets the rebound and moves (you decide) back to his team and hands the ball to the next player.

This is a fantastic game because it accounts for the youngsters who can't shoot; they can still score points for the team by bowling. By adding a second ball into the game you can improve the movement time and decrease the waiting time. By

GAME 6-26. BASKETBOWL (continued)

changing a component or categories you can design dozens more games using the basic framework. I allow the teams to develop strategies for getting the ball quickly to each teammate. This game can be played in a relatively small gym. To provide for less confusion at the shooting area, it is suggested that you set the gym up in the following manner:

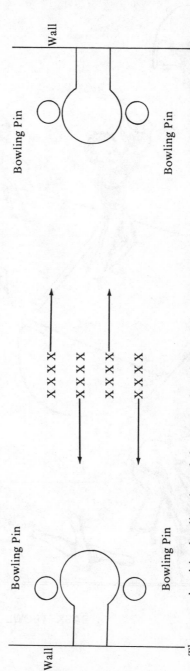

The teams bowl in the direction of the arrows but shoot at the other end of the gym. This eliminates four people at the same basket at the same time.

BASKETBOWL

GAME 6-27. BOUNCE BALL (SECONDARY)

Players	Equipment	Movements	Organ. Pattern	Limitations	Purpose
7 per team	1 large ball, 1 small ball	running passing hopping	random	1. Must one-hand-dribble ball in selected areas. 2. Must hop while dribbling ball in marked area. 3. One point for ball through basket in traditional manner; 3 points if you can bounce ball into basket. Double points using small ball. 4. Game over when 15 points are scored. 5. Play both balls independently of one another.	To develop shooting and passing skills.

Description: There are 7 players on the court from each team at the same time. The game is conducted much like traditional basketball but with more players and different types of balls, additional rules and additional hopping movement.

GAME 6-28. HOCKEY BALL (SECONDARY)

Players	Equipment	Movements	Organ. Pattern	Limitations	Purpose
5-8 per team	2 balls, 2 bats, 4 lummey sticks	running, dribbling, shooting	random	1. Play both balls independently of one another. 2. The lummey sticks are used to dribble the balls in specifically marked areas by hitting the balls with the sticks. 3. Each team has one bat and is allowed to stand under its own basket and by sticking the bat up through the net, may try to prevent a ball from going through. 4. Bat may only be held vertically by one player in specially marked area beneath defensive basket. 5. Four points for each basket; time limit game, you decide.	To develop shooting, passing strategy skills

Description: Each team gets 1 ball, 1 bat and 2 lummey sticks. The game is much like traditional basketball except that in designated areas the ball must be dribbled via lummey sticks. Balls may be blocked by a goalie with a bat positioned up through the net. All other traditional basketball skills may be employed.

HOCKEY BALL

GAME 6-29. BACK-TO-BACK BASKETBALL (SECONDARY)

Players	Equipment	Movements	Organ. Pattern	Limitations	Purpose
any number up to 7 per team	2 balls per game	all regular basketball movements	random	1. Use 2 basketball courts which are back-to-back, see diagram. 2. Each team gets one ball, both balls are put into play at same time. 3. Must shoot at basket not facing your team at beginning of game. 4. To begin game each team lines up facing basket they will defend (see diagram). 5. Regular basketball rules are then followed. After a score you must take ball out-of-bounds at mid-court of your own defensive basket.	To develop basketball skills. To promote problem solving.

Description: The only differences between this game and the traditional game is that 2 balls are used and you use 2 baskets that are back to back. All basketball skills are used. After a basket has been made, the ball must be returned to original start position before being thrown in again. Usually plastic cones or mid-court lines designate this boundary.

The back-to-back basketball game became a favorite among several of my high school senior classes. They adjusted the rules as they needed to. Most important, they decided upon the rule changes prior to beginning play.

With each of the previously described games, the door is open for change. Oftentimes the students will ask you for certain types of equipment, things that may appear to be "junk." Our school did not have a large physical education equipment budget; as a matter of fact we usually received the athletic rejects (equipment). Thus we made every effort to find a use for each and every item we had. Instead of discarding broken bats, the students found an effective use for them. Many students started to bring their "junk" equipment to school. It became quite a challenge to the students to figure out (solve a problem) how to incorporate the "equipment" into a game. The students would use various types of balls not traditionally meant to be used in the sport of basketball. They used everything from small plastic balls to basketball bladders extracted from worn out basketballs. Many times the students would use regulation basketballs in combination with other types of balls.

Can you think of some other ways to alter the traditional game? You can see that most of the changes made by the students occurred in the Equipment, Movement, and Organizational Pattern categories. By trial and error and by logical thinking the students developed a multitude of games that they found enjoyable to play. Many of the students began to think about game strategy and category relationship for the first time.

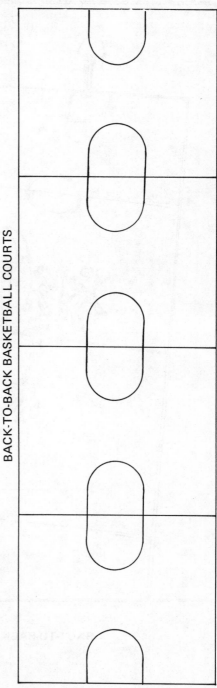

BACK-TO-BACK BASKETBALL COURTS

BACK-TO-BACK BASKETBALL

ACTIVE ACADEMIC GAMES

Drs. James Humphrey* and Bryant Cratty** have developed a category of games that requires basic academic operations to be performed within a movement structure. Their books are excellent and highly recommended for use by elementary classroom teachers, special education teachers, and by physical educators. The major thesis of their books is games of movement that require specific kinds of cognitive operations to be of value to children. The games are not an educational cure-all and should not be used to replace more familiar methods of teaching academic subjects. Both authors suggest that the games be used as supplemental aids to classroom teachers.

This author has been using these active games for the past six years and has found that they do indeed have a place within the educational community. The following games are representative of Cratty's active learning games. Application of the games analysis process, however, demonstrates how it is also possible to modify these games to meet your students' needs.

MEMORY GAMES

Short-term serial memory is a most necessary skill for children to possess. Not only is this a prerequisite to other cognitive operations, but it is necessary for daily survival. How many times have you given these kinds of directions to a young child: "John, please go to the office and get three pencils, a ream of paper, a bottle of glue, and some staples. Bring these items back to me—thank you." And John returns with the pencils and the staples, having forgotten the other two items. A teacher may make some unnecessary remarks to John, unaware that maybe his auditory short-term memory needs some work. Let's examine some visual and auditory short-term memory games.

---

*James Humphrey and Dorothy Sullivan, *Teaching Slow Learners through Active Games* (Springfield, Illinois: Charles C. Thomas, 1970).
**Bryant Cratty, *Active Learning* (Englewood Cliffs, N.J.: Prentice Hall, 1971) and *Intelligence in Action* (Prentice-Hall, 1973).

GAME 6-30.

STAY BEHIND (Visual Short-Term Memory Game)

Players	Equipment	Movements	Organ. Pattern	Limitations	Purpose
unlimited	none, or any piece of equipment desired, so long as every player has access to the equipment at the same time	unlimited nonlocomotor locomotor propulsion reception movements	random scatter in front of the games leader	1. Players must simply stay one or more moves behind the move demonstrated by the games leader. 2. Games leader starts game over when several players have missed. 3. No one is ever eliminated.	Enhance short-term visual memory.

Description: Games leader performs movement A, players memorize movement A. Leader performs movement B, now players perform movement A. This is repeated, players always staying one move behind the leader. The leader can perform exercises, e.g., ball-handling skills, or any physical movement he or she desires. This game is similar to Cratty's One Behind except the author has added other kinds of movements.

GAME 6-31.

COUPLES RACES *(Auditory Short-Term Memory Game)*

Players	Equipment	Movements	Organ. Pattern	Limitations	Purpose
partners	none or any piece of equipment can be used	nonlocomotor locomotor reception propulsion movements	2 lines facing one another—partners opposite each other X - - - - 0 X - - - - 0 X - - - - 0 X - - - - 0	1. Games leader gives movement tasks to one set of players (X's). 2. Start by giving players 3 tasks. 3. Object of game is, on start signal, for X's to perform all 3 tasks as quickly as possible and return to sitting position when they are completed. 4. Don't name winners—race is over when *everyone* is back and sitting down. 5. Increase degree of difficulty by giving 4, 5, 6 tasks in a series.	To enhance short-term auditory memory.

Description: Games leader gives one set of partners (X's) 3 tasks to perform in or around their partners (O's). For example: you must run around your partner, crawl through his legs, and jump over him. Race is over when everyone is back sitting down. This game can be repeated with other partners performing. How many versions can you think of?

MATH GAMES

Many elementary teachers find it difficult at times to keep an active class interested in specific math concepts. The following games suggest how a teacher can positively improve the class need for movement by designing math games that require a great deal of energy expenditure. Remember, you can incorporate any math concept or operation into one of the following games, or you can develop your own math games by this point in the book.

GAME 6-32. ALL 4's CIRCLE MATH

Players	Equipment	Movements	Organ. Pattern	Limitations	Purpose
5-8 per team	none or limited	running jumping crawling dribbling you name it!	Each team is lying on the floor in a circle, heads towards the center of the circle (make sure teams aren't too close to one another).	1. Each player is assigned a number. 2. Game leader provides a math problem (e.g., $2 + \_\_ = 4$). 3. The players in each group fill in the blank with the correct number. 4. The person who is the correct number must get up, jump over each player in the group, and return to start position.	Enhance addition, subtraction, multiplication, division skills.

Description: Players are lying on the floor and each child in each group has been assigned a number. Games leader gives all the groups a math problem (e.g., $2 + 2 = \_\_$). The answer gets up, jumps over everyone in his/her group, and returns to start position. *Variations*: Assign every child more than one number. Perform subtraction, multiplication and division problems. Have children move in relationship to other groups. Use equipment. Have several children move at the same time in the same group.

GAME 6-33. MULTIPLICATION BALANCE

Players	Equipment	Movements	Organ. Pattern	Limitations	Purpose
5-8 per team	small equipment large equipment grid bean bags	unlimited	Teams can be in standard file, relay pattern, or facing a learning grid.	1. Time limit game (3 minutes long. 2. One member at a time from each team has an opportunity to throw a bean bag onto learning grid. 3. Number that the bag lands on becomes the multiplier on team multiplication sheet. 4. After placing number on sheet and completing the problem, player moves the balance beam, walks backwards on beam (if player doesn't fall, add 5 to score sheet). 5. First team to reach 300 wins game.	To enhance multiplication and balance skills.

Description: Each team sends one player at a time to the learning grid area. After throwing a bean bag onto the grid, the player fills in the team's multiplication sheet, proceeds to balance beam area, walks on one of the beams, and returns to own team. Next player goes after preceding player has returned to the team. Sample score sheet:

2 X   =
3 X   =
4 X   =

(Learning grids can be made from painter's drop cloth and the numbers from contact paper.)

MULTIPLICATION BALANCE

GAME 6-34. HOMOPHONE SHOT

Players	Equipment	Movements	Organ. Pattern	Limitations	Purpose
6-9 per team	basketball for every team, jump rope for every team	shooting jumping rope running	spokes of the wheel	1. Team with most homophone pairs wins. 2. One player at a time runs to center of organizational circle, picks up homophone pair. 3. Player moves to basket, has one opportunity to shoot, score 3 points. 4. Team with most points also wins. 5. Time limit game (3 minutes).	Work on homophone pairs. Develop basketball shooting skills.

Description: One player at a time moves to homophone cards. Upon locating a pair, player moves to basketball shooting area and has only one opportunity to score a basket. Player then returns to team.

HOMOPHONE SHOT

LANGUAGE COMMUNICATION
GAMES

A great deal of every school day is devoted to language communication skills such as reading, writing, and grammar. Active learning games can be designed to accommodate the many different reading methodologies that currently exist. Most reading specialists indicate that children must learn to read by attaching meaning to symbols, the left-right principle as well as many other concepts. By using games analysis strategies it is possible to develop your own reading games. The following games illustrate this idea.

GAME 6-35. NOUN, ADJECTIVE, VERB POTPOURRI

Players	Equipment	Movements	Organ. Pattern	Limitations	Purpose
6-8 per team	balance beams jump ropes tumbling mats	running jumping rolling balancing	Spokes of the wheel, teams face center of circle Balance beams are placed in center of circle. Jump ropes are behind team.	1. Within each team, a player becomes a noun, adjective or verb. 2. One player at a time per team walks a balance beam (placed in front of team) until player reaches a story printed on a sheet of paper. 3. Player quickly reads story and circles part of speech that he or she is. 4. Player must run to jump rope (placed behind team) and jump rope 10 times. 5. Player must move to nearest mat, roll like a ball. 6. Next player leaves from team when preceding player starts jumping rope. 7. Time limit game (4 minutes). When game is over, check answers.	Enhance language communication skills. Allow practice time for selected motor skills.

Description: The games teacher prints a story or paragraphs from a story on a sheet of paper (probably a story worked on previously in class). Players must circle the correct part of speech (only one word at a time) as they read the story (if a player is a noun, player tries to find a noun in story). I have the children not only circle the proper word but indicate above the word what part of speech it is. After they complete this part of the game, player must complete other movement tasks. You can ask the children to perform any movement task they have previously performed.

NOUN, ADJECTIVE, VERB POTPOURRI

Chapter

7

Some
Closing Thoughts

All teachers bring to their classes a set of beliefs and a set of biases regarding *what* should be taught and *how* it should be taught. Each one of us wants to repeat our successes and eliminate our failures as we teach day to day. Certainly at the elementary school level an important part of the physical education curriculum is an area known as games. All of us have our own opinion as to their worth in the total development of our students. Some of us teach games for recreation purposes while others of us teach games for specific motoric reasons. Regardless of what we think games can do for youngsters, it is absolutely imperative that we understand that games must be designed in specific ways in order for certain behaviors to result. Hoping that a youngster will become a "better sport" and/or saying that a game enhances emotional self-confidence is like trying to drive from Los Angeles to Death Valley in mid-July without any water in the car. You find out partway through your journey that you forgot a most important item—water. It is the same way with games; if the teacher has not carefully structured the game, partway through the game it turns out that an item is missing—the design of the game is mandating the behavioral outcome. I believe that teachers must reevaluate the role of games in an elementary physical education class in light of the objectives stated for the class and that teachers need to understand the relationships between game designs and behavioral outcomes if they want *each* youngster to develop to his or her capacity within a game environment. This statement presupposes that all teachers realize that youngsters develop physically, emotionally, socially, and intellectually at various rates but in similar patterns. It also presupposes that all teachers are aware of the stages of development. This book has attempted to describe briefly the developmental stages through which youngsters seem to progress, and, through the medium of games, to share with you some ideas on how to structure games in order to account for individual differences. It is hoped that as a result you will question the role, use, and value of certain game designs. You see, it is not necessarily essential that elementary youngsters learn *the way* to hand dribble a regulation basketball or perform an instep kick in soccer. An elementary program's sole responsibility is not necessarily to prepare youngsters for junior and senior high movement physical education game and sport programs. Rather, sequencing motor patterns or movement behaviors for individual youngsters should be considered just as important as learning specific sports skills.

Terry Orlick* has written an excellent book on cooperative games that allow all children to enjoy the fun experiences of games. An example of these games is one he designed called "cooperative musical chairs." The game is played like regular musical chairs, but as the chairs are eliminated the players must share the remaining chairs with one another. The players learn how to cooperate and share with others. If you have not read his book or articles, please do—you will find yet another games approach available to you.

Vern Seefeldt (1972) at Michigan State University has spent years developing a curriculum for elementary youngsters that attempts to sequence movements for youngsters. It is important to have a tool to exhibit this idea. Hopefully, games analysis begins to allow teachers to skillfully sequence movement activities within the games movement environment.

It is also important to deal with the whole child rather than attempt to segregate a youngster's life into separate entities. Thus it is our role to concern ourselves with the emotional, social, and intellectual development of our youngsters. No longer can we say that it is someone else's job to teach youngsters how to cooperate, how to express inner feelings, how to compete, how to employ

---

*Terry Orlick, *The Cooperative Sports and Games Book* (New York: Pantheon Books, 1978).

human relation strategies—it is the role of *every* teacher. When someone says to me that education should be a reflection of the real world, I first ask why, and secondly I ask him to state in specific observable behaviors what he means. You see, I am not sure that many of us can find the handle on identifying specific behaviors. Games analysis in its very limited fashion is an attempt to provide the teacher with a tool that helps identify behaviors and teach to those same behaviors.

Finally, youngsters must be involved in rational decision-making processes. Making decisions and realizing that there are consequences to the decisions made is a learned behavior. Because decision making involves a process, this suggests that teachers have a tool they can use to develop each youngster's decision-making ability. Games analysis, limited as it is, attempts to provide the teacher with a tool to use in developing this ability.

Games are important to youngsters and adults. Let us critically analyze their use in physical education programs. Let us realize that games, in and of themselves, should not be *the* curriculum for our programs, rather games represent only one of the mediums through which youngsters learn about themselves. Perhaps we need to investigate the entire structure of our curriculum in light of "Are we really consistent in our curriculum design and the outcomes expected from its design?" Perhaps our educational beliefs are not really properly reflected in the types of movement experiences we provide for our students. This is why I think that it is most important to understand what games can do for and do against youngsters. Yes, it is time to know How to Change the Games Children Play.

References

Seefeldt, Vern. "Sequencing Motor Skills within the Physical Education Curriculum." Paper presented at AAHPER National Convention, Houston, Texas, March 27, 1972.

Mosston, Muska. *Teaching Physical Education.* Columbus, Ohio: Charles E. Merrill Publishing Co., 1966.

Appendix

Factors and Choices *

CATCHING

	Color of Ball	Background Color	Speed of Flight
Easy	blue	white	10 m.p.h.
↓	yellow	black	15 m.p.h.
	orange	black	20 m.p.h.
	red	white	25 m.p.h.
	green	yellow	30 m.p.h.
Difficult	??	??	??

	Angle of Trajectory	Texture of Ball
Easy	Horizontal	soft — balloon, beach ball, nerf ball
	Vertical	firm — playground ball, bladder of balls, rubber balls
	Arc	hard — softballs, whiffle balls, baseballs, ??
	???	
Difficult		

*The factors shown here are by no means all that influence these movement behaviors. They represent examples, and readers are invited to share their ideas with us.

KICKING

	Position of Ball Movement	Type of Kick
Easy	stationary	toe kick
	horizontally rolling	instep kick
	bouncing roll	punt
	ball in flight	outside foot kick
Difficult	??	??

	Texture of Ball	Shape of Object	Anticipation Location
Easy	beachball	cardboard box	no step and kick
	playground ball	milk carton	take a step - kick
	all purpose ball	round ball	take 3 steps - kick
	soccer ball	oblong ball	run distance - kick
	football	??	??
Difficult	??		

JUMPING

	Type of Jump	Landing Surface	Body Position
Easy	jump down	crash pads	compact
	horizontal jump	saw dust pit	
	vertical jump	gym mat	extended
	??	concrete surface	??
Difficult		??	

BODY ROLLING

	Body Position	Body Speed while Rolling	Direction of Roll
Easy	compact	slow	forward
↓	tucked	↓	sideways
	curled		backwards
	piked		??
Difficult	extended	fast	
	??	??	

	Initiation Height of Roll	Distance From Start Point to Roll Initiation
Easy	close to mat-squat	1 ft.
↓	bent over position	2 ft.
	standing position	3 ft.
Difficult	jump to roll	5 ft.
	??	??